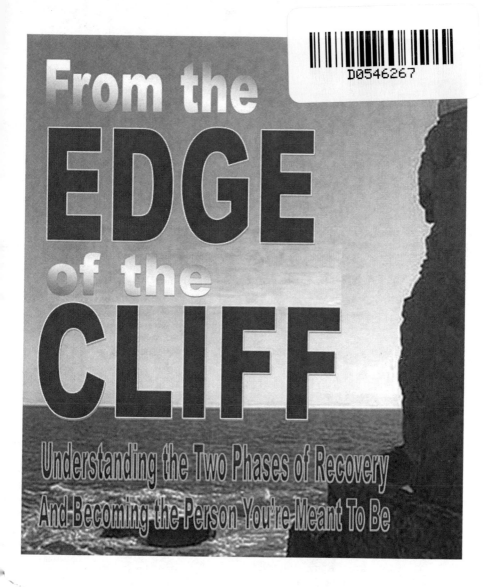

From the EDGE of the CLIFF

Understanding the Two Phases of Recovery And Becoming the Person You're Meant To Be

Dawn V. Obrecht, M.D.

✝RICHER Press
An Imprint of Richer Life, LLC

ALSO BY

Dawn V. Obrecht, M.D.

MISSION POSSIBLE
A Missionary Doctor's Journey of Healing

"Mission Possible" Has Been Nominated For a
2012 Montaigne Medal

The Montaigne Medal

Each year, the Eric Hoffer Award for books presents the Montaigne Medal to the most thought-provoking title(s). These are books that either illuminate, progress, or redirect thought. The Montaigne Medal is given in honor of the great French philosopher Michel de Montaigne, who influenced people such as William Shakespeare, René Descartes, Ralph Waldo Emerson, Friedrich Nietzsche, Jean-Jacques Rousseau, and Eric Hoffer.

Montaigne Medal
Eric Hoffer Award
Excellence in
Independent Publishing

Copyright © 2012 by Richer Life, LLC

Published by ‡RICHER Press
An Imprint of Richer Life, LLC

4600 E. Washington Street, Suite 300, Phoenix, Arizona 85034
www.richerlifeassociates.com

Twelve Steps reprinted for adaptation by permission of AA World Services, Inc.
Reprinted from the Little White Booklet, Narcotics Anonymous. © 1986 by Narcotics
Anonymous World Services, Inc., PO Box 9999, Van Nuys, CA 91409 ISBN 0-912075-
65-1 10/00

Cover Design: Richer Media USA • Photographs: Big Stock Photo

Library of Congress Cataloging-in-Publications Data

From the Edge of the Cliff:
Understanding the Two Phases of Recovery
And Becoming the Person You're Meant To Be
Dawn V. Obrecht, M.D. -- 1st edition
p.   cm.

1. Addiction & Recovery   2. Addiction Medicine   3. Chemical Dependency
ISBN 978-0-9744617-9-3 (pbk : alk. Paper)

2012933804

ISBN 13: 978-0-9744617-9-3

ISBN 10: 0-9744617-9-3

Text set is Adobe Garamond

PRINTED IN THE UNITED STATES OF AMERICA

First edition
April 2012

DEDICATION

This book is dedicated to my husband, Erik Landvik.

Thank you for believing in me, encouraging me and loving me.

I thank God for giving us to each other.

CONTENTS

ACKNOWLEDGEMENTS

Thank you, Scott, for encouraging me to "follow in my mother's footsteps and write", and for doing it again when I did not respond the first time. Thank you to the staff of *The Local,* for publishing every article I wrote, no matter how controversial and inflammatory, for over three years. Those articles make up the backbone of this book and are still available in their original form at www.docdawn.com.

Kevin, my enormous gratitude goes to you for working with me to connect the dots and transform my assorted writings into one manuscript. Earl and Char, I thank God, and everyone at Impact Church in Scottsdale, Arizona, for putting you in my life at just the right time so you could take my manuscript to the next level and turn it into this book. *Coincidence* is just one of God's pennames.

Thank you to my wonderful patients, coworkers, friends and family for continuing to teach me that God is in charge and everything happens just exactly as it is supposed to happen. I am especially thankful for my daughters, Brie and Kara, and their husbands, Dave and Sven. While you may think my next endeavor is the craziest yet, and you sometimes complain that I am always busy, you are consistently supportive. Thanks for letting me be your mom, mom-in-law and oma to the best grandchildren on the face of the earth, Alex, Owen, Bergen, Ahren and Tova!

Most of all, thank you to my husband Erik Landvik. Whew! What is the next adventure? You stand by me and help me to have the courage to be true to myself and not be quieted by what others may think. Your continued love and support is more that I could have imagined when we met at the Gilpin Street Uptown Steppers meeting in 1988. Without you, my life would be dull at best.

AUTHOR'S NOTE

You will note that I have opted to use the words "addict" and "alcoholic" almost interchangeably, as alcoholics are simply alcohol addicts. Some alcoholics use only alcohol, but many use other mind-altering drugs and processes. I emphasize being completely drug free, whether you call yourself alcoholic or addict. To that end, I also use the terms "clean" and "sober" together and interchangeably, knowing there is an element of redundancy. If this is inconsistent with your own reference points, I invite you to mentally substitute your own language.

While I am keenly aware that there are members of both NA and AA who sometimes bristle at the crossover of the terms, "alcoholic" and "addict", "clean" and "sober", I have written this book for a wide audience and attempted to be inclusive. In my own journey of 28 years in recovery I have been blessed by being offered inclusion, acceptance and love in all fellowships. I wish the same for you.

Dawn V. Obrecht, M.D.

Addiction

(American Society of Addiction Medicine, April 2011)

Addiction is a primary, chronic disease of brain reward, motivation, memory and related circuitry. Dysfunction in these circuits leads to characteristic biological, psychological, social and spiritual manifestations. This is reflected in an individual pathologically pursuing reward and/or relief by substance use and other behaviors.

Addiction is characterized by inability to consistently abstain, impairment in behavioral control, craving, diminished recognition of significant problems with one's behaviors and interpersonal relationships, and a dysfunctional emotional response. Like other chronic diseases, addiction often involves cycles of relapse and remission. Without treatment or engagement in recovery activities, addiction is progressive and can result in disability or premature death.

[The "Long Version" of this definition can be found on Page 247]

INTRODUCTION

At the time, it seemed like a perfectly natural set of choices. If you are an addict or know one, maybe you can relate.

Choice #1: Get up early on a crisp autumn Colorado morning, climb in the car with my two girls, ages 6 and 3, take a little drive up that steep Rocky Mountain road near our home. Then, find one of those spots among the hairpin turns with the gorgeous views, and, after making sure none of us is wearing a seat belt or secured in a car seat, drive the car full speed off the 1,000-foot cliff. That would finally put an end to the anger, pain, and anxiety that all the alcohol and drugs that I could consume just couldn't cover up anymore, and it would ease my conscience knowing that I would not be leaving my daughters Brie and Kara behind.

Choice #2: Sign up for a five-day medical education conference in Denver to gain the Continuing Ed credits to maintain my hospital staff privileges. I could drink as much as I wanted because I'd be staying in a hotel and would not have to go home at night and pretend to be a responsible mother. Oh, and maybe I'd sign up for that section on alcohol and addiction. You never know, I might even learn something—about my father and mother's drinking problem.

Thank God, something, some power greater than me, steered me to Choice #2. Did I drink during those three days and nights? You bet. But I did show up for that afternoon panel on addiction, presented by a warm, personable physician named Blair Carlson. And when Dr. Carlson finished his slide show, my eyes fixated on the final panel of his professional credits: Graduate, Pier I Treatment Center. After his talk I joined the many attendees gathered around him, and when it was my turn in line he made clear, direct eye contact with me. Something in that look pulled me in. I asked if I could visit his treatment center, and several days later, after the tour, he asked me if I had any questions.

"It's been very helpful to see what you have here because I have some friends who may have problems with cocaine," I began, already choking back the tears. "And…maybe…that is…well…I think I might have a problem too."

"Of course you do," he replied calmly. "Why else would you be here?"

And on that pivotal day in October 1983 I dissolved into a pile of tears on this wise, compassionate doctor's floor. I spilled more details of my story: the terror and shame of growing up in a verbally abusive, alcoholic home; my own out-of-control addicted life; my two suicide attempts; reaching for my stash of cocaine in the kitchen microwave while watching my two little girls. I wish I could say I went home that very night and threw out all my alcohol, cocaine, and every other drug tucked in every corner of my home, never to use again. The truth was, Halloween was coming. I mean, how could I take on my favorite holiday without snorting a few lines? Neighborhood parents typically carried cups for liquid treats while we took our children from house to house; how could I miss out on that? Oh, and soon it would be Thanksgiving and December, with my birthday and Christmas, and on to New Year's—how could anyone not drink on New Year's Eve? It took me until the following March to get clean, but once I made that choice I never looked back. A few weeks ago I celebrated my 28th anniversary of recovery.

I have faced barrels full of new and difficult choices along the way, and while I sure haven't made 100 per cent of the clear and healthy ones, I know that my decisions today are guided by emotionally and spiritually healthy thinking. I have plenty to celebrate every day. I have a rich spiritual life that includes a relationship with God that sustains me. My daughters, Brie and Kara, are now healthy and vibrant adults with husbands I cherish having in our family and I have five grandchildren, the first two of whom I got to deliver. I am married to a wonderful man who understands the road to recovery because he has been on his own journey almost as long as I have. At 63, I am fit enough to compete in triathlons and travel the world to serve on medical missions. I have dozens of wonderful friends, many drawn from the worldwide community of Alcoholics Anonymous and Narcotics Anonymous that have served as the bedrock of my recovery.

And today, as an MD Addictionist for more than 20 years, and a Fellow of the American Society of Addiction Medicine, I am doing the work I love. I help addicts and their families, as well as healthcare professionals, better understand and navigate the frightening and confusing world of addiction and recovery and its close relative, "DFS", Dysfunctional Family Syndrome. That is my mission, my passion. And that's what this book is all about.

If you are an addict struggling to break free from the ball and chain of addiction, I offer critical information, encouragement, and hope, from someone who's been there. I'm fond of T-shirts with messages, and one of my favorites is "The Lie Is Dead—We Do Recover." I see the evidence every day in my practice and in the Twelve Step meetings I still enthusiastically attend everywhere I go. Alcohol and drug addiction are more prevalent than ever, but no matter how desperate your life situation may feel today, recovery is available to you. The way out, or the way through, is right within your grasp. I'm here to assure you that it is possible for you to not only survive addiction but to thrive in a life of recovery. Riding through this crazy, painful, turbulent storm and coming out intact can open a door to a life of peace, joy, and service to others and the world.

We will be exploring the path of recovery through concise, easy-to-follow, practical lessons that will inform and inspire you about many of the most pressing choices and challenges you will encounter. These tips and reminders are divided into what I call Phase I Recovery and Phase II Recovery. In my nearly three decades of personal and professional experience, I have come to recognize how the needs and possibilities of recovery change and evolve over time. Understanding the distinctions between these two phases and learning how to identify where you are and what is called for in each period will help you to navigate the trail more successfully and harmoniously.

In Phase I Recovery, your focus is on finding your way out of addiction. You've reached the starting gate to the rest of your life, a life that hopefully will remain free of alcohol and other drugs. Your overriding goal is to stay clean, and your energy is mostly directed toward the logistics of recovery: attending recovery meetings, following the Twelve Steps, keeping drugs out of reach, steering clear of the people who still use them, doing whatever you can to avoid a relapse, etc. As you map your course of recovery, you discover that you need to practice whole new ways of thinking and behaving if you want to claim physical, emotional, and spiritual health. You must look with fresh eyes on how you got where you are and what it will take to get where you need to go. It's a turbulent time when recovery often feels fragile, requiring all your effort to hang on. And yet, you also begin to see and experience the profound benefits of being free of addiction.

Then, perhaps six months or a year or two along the recovery trail, you notice a shift. You're no longer spending most of your time and energy fighting to stay clean, anxious that a relapse is lurking around every corner, and overwhelmed by the seemingly never-ending demands of figuring out how to act and what to do without drugs and everything that went with them. Life may not be easy but it's easier. Old habits have faded away, and more productive habits have sprung up. Your feet are on the ground, you've rejoined the mainstream of society, and you feel more comfortable with yourself more often. For many addicts in recovery, this plateau is the ground on which they remain. It's "as good as it gets." But most of us notice that something is still missing, some intangible piece to the recovery story that leaves us feeling sad or lost. We sense, even if we can't put words to it, that somewhere underneath what may feel like our empty self there lays the desire we all have: to find inner peace, to build real physical, emotional, and spiritual health, to not only claim freedom from the destructive behavior of addiction but to enjoy the kind of life we're all meant to live and deserve to have. We want something more...we hunger for a Phase II Recovery.

You can find many resources and books that tell dramatic stories about hitting rock bottom and taking that first courageous step toward life, but scant few that explore what happens in the next scene. We're going to look behind that curtain. In Phase II Recovery we'll cover tools on staying the course and explore how to change the story of your painful and destructive past. We'll take on the final frontier of relationships. I'll invite you to expand your horizons about what is possible in this next part of the journey, when life can actually feel good and you are able to appreciate it so much more. I'll help you continue your own path toward becoming the person you're meant to be.

If you are an addict who has tapped, or is on the verge of summoning the strength, courage, and faith to begin your recovery, congratulations! Making it through Phase I Recovery is the most important work you will ever do, so we will be spending extra time

16

there. If you have remained clean for several months, or even many years, but yearn for "something more," I urge you not to skip too quickly over the lessons of Phase I Recovery because this journey will always be about doing and re-doing the basics. Then, when you read the new perspectives and inspiring ideas and accounts in Phase II Recovery, my hope is that you will have an "aha" that propels you to climb higher.

If you have a loved one struggling with addiction, I know that you too are suffering. Addicts do immeasurable harm to those around them, as well as to themselves, and you confront your own hard choices, with no easy answers, every day. Take heart; you are not alone. As I hope you already know, there is also help for you, free, in the Twelve Step programs, and you will find invaluable ideas and illustrations in the pages ahead. Many lessons are written just for you.

There's one other vital and often missed piece to the recovery puzzle we will be unraveling in Part 2: "Beware, Your Doctor May be Your Pusher!" As an addiction specialist who treats and counsels addicts every day, I see consistent evidence that when it comes to detecting and treating addiction, doctors all too often wind up as part of the problem rather than part of the solution. If you happen to be a physician, therapist, or other healthcare provider, I have the utmost respect for the hard work and dedication it takes to achieve your profession and practice medicine or therapy. But the simple truth is far too many doctors know far too little about addicts and their recovery. I will point out the most common misunderstandings and mistakes doctors make, so you addicts can be forewarned and you doctors may be informed.

When I teach practicing physicians, medical students, interns, and nurses about addiction and recovery, I'm always gratified when they begin to relate to addicts with the breadth of knowledge and understanding it takes to help those in such dire need—those who also can be very difficult to work with! But we've got a long, long way to go. Health care professionals everywhere must learn more about the disease of addiction—where it comes from, what it looks like, and how to nurture the long, delicate process of recovery. If I sound tough on you at times, my fellow doctors, please understand that my words come from a place of respect, compassion, and the desire to help this cause as best as I know how. Disagree as you may, but I sincerely invite your ear and your consideration.

As you read through the book, feel free to tune in to the lessons that most speak to you, and leave the rest. I will sprinkle in snapshots from my own experience, as well as others I have known or worked with, because what we gain from hearing others who have been there trumps anything we hear from anyone else. And oh boy, have I been there!

One of my most vivid childhood memories is awakening in the night and rushing to the top of the stairs to see my father backing my mother into a corner with a large, dusty pink upholstered chair. As he screamed obscenities at her, my mother, hands covering her face, pleaded with him to stop. Years later, Mom confided to me that one day when I was 3 and having a little girl tantrum at the top of the wooden stairs to the basement of our Baltimore row house, she imagined pushing me down so I would crash into the cement floor. Then, free of the responsibility of motherhood, she could finally leave him. But she didn't push me. She became an alcoholic herself instead.

One night, when I was 12, I consumed the contents of every medication I could get my hands on at our home, and when I woke up, I was angry to find myself still alive. That same year I decided that I would become a doctor—if I couldn't cure my parents, maybe I could cure somebody else. Two years later I started drinking. I was off and running on a 20-year trail of addiction that almost drove me off that cliff. Along the way, I made another attempt to kill myself with an overdose of drugs—while training to be a doctor. Want to know one of the craziest parts of my addictive life? For most of those two decades of abusing alcohol and drugs, I was in therapy. But none of those health care professionals—not the school psychologists at college or in medical school, and not the psychiatrist whose couch I lied on every week, up to four times a week, during eight years of extensive therapy as a practicing physician and mother—ever confronted me with my addiction. Is it any wonder that I'm so passionate about helping not only addicts but the doctors and therapists who see them every day?

Building and sustaining Phase I Recovery and opening to the rich possibilities of Phase II Recovery requires a series of hard, deliberate choices, and even harder work. In whatever phase you may happen to be, I suspect you know that. In making those tough choices, you may be calling upon Twelve Step recovery groups, therapists who understand addiction, your church or other religious or spiritual support system, loved ones who support you, and a whole other cast of valuable allies. That's great, because you can never have too many "mates," or helpers. My hope is to be one of those mates, one more resource to strengthen your chances of claiming that healthy and enriched life you are meant to live. One more anchor to guide you through the tough choices. If I can in any way contribute to you choosing and continuing along the right path, I will consider myself blessed many times over.

So, are you ready for the first lesson?

Congratulations! It takes extraordinary courage to claim recovery as your new way of living.

PART I

PHASE I RECOVERY: FINDING THE WAY OUT

Addicts who have succeeded in recovery know one vital truth: what you do in the first several weeks and months of recovery will have a whole lot to do with your chances of making it over the long haul.

SECTION 1: MAPPING THE NEW TERRAIN

Lesson #1
LEARN AND FOLLOW
THE TWELVE STEPS

So you've chosen to embark on a recovery program. You're poised to break the cycle of addiction in your life, and if you come from a family plagued by addiction you have a chance to break an even larger cycle. Congratulations! It takes extraordinary courage to claim recovery as your new way of living. And whether you saw through the fog of denial through your own choice or whether you got smacked into the wall of reality by one dramatic, painful episode, it doesn't matter. You're here. You have an opportunity to move forward in Phase I Recovery. You can find your way out of addiction.

Addicts who have succeeded in recovery know one vital truth: what you do in the first several weeks and months of recovery will have a whole lot to do with your chances of making it over the long haul. Phase I Recovery comes wrapped in a slew of tough choices and potential land mines. We're going to take them on, one by one. This first series of lessons will help you navigate the dangerous terrain, to steer you toward a safe and healthy passage. I'll help you map this new course and look out for slip-ups as you do the hard work that recovery demands. I'll also provide concrete tips and ideas for how to begin to claim physical, emotional, and spiritual health and well-being as you walk this new path.

Phase I Recovery is rich with the potential for starting to transform your life, planting the seeds that can grow into a vibrant Phase II Recovery. So buckle down and read carefully.

I know of only one way to begin these lessons that can save your life, and that is to point you toward the resource that saved my own life and has saved countless thousands of others: the Twelve Steps** of Alcoholics Anonymous, Narcotics Anonymous, and their 120-plus related recovery programs. No matter what other resources you may choose to call upon, the Twelve Steps can and should serve as a solid foundation.

You can find the Twelve Steps, and everything else you need to know about AA, NA, and other Twelve Step programs, on the websites: www.aa.org and www.na.org. Here is how the 12 Steps of by Narcotics Anonymous read:

1) We admitted we were powerless over our addiction—that our lives had become unmanageable.

2) We came to believe that a Power greater than ourselves could restore us to sanity.

3) We made a decision to turn our will and our lives over to the care of God as we understood Him.

4) We made a searching and fearless moral inventory of ourselves.

5) We admitted to God, to ourselves, and to another human being the exact nature of our wrongs.

6) We were entirely ready to have God remove all these defects of character.

7) We humbly asked Him to remove our shortcomings.

8) We made a list of all persons we had harmed and became willing to make amends to them all.

9) We made direct amends to such people wherever possible, except when to do so would injure them or others.

10) We continued to take personal inventory and when we were wrong promptly admitted it.

11) We sought through prayer and meditation to improve our conscious contact with God as we understood Him, praying only for knowledge of His will for us and the power to carry that out.

12) Having had a spiritual awakening as the result of these steps, we tried to carry this message to addicts, and to practice these principles in all our affairs.

The Twelve Steps may be well known throughout our culture today, but it amazes and frustrates me when I see so many addicts in need try to convince themselves that they can get clean and stay clean while completely sidestepping them. Their attempts almost always fail.

Here's just one example. Danny was so resistant to recovery when I first saw him as a patient and diagnosed his addiction that I gave him a copy of the AA Big Book and took him to an AA meeting myself. A year later I heard that he had been in court for a DUI and had even done time in jail. I reached out to him via email. "How are you doing, Danny?" I asked. "I'm fine," he replied. Well, I wasn't so sure of that, and I wanted to show my ongoing support. So I sent him periodic follow-up emails, and each time he would write back: "I'm fine." When I ran into him in a parking lot in our town, I walked right up to him and his four-year-old boy. Looking Danny in the eyes, I said, "How ARE you?" He responded, "I'm fine...no, I'm not really fine."

He admitted he was drinking again. "But I don't want to do this anymore. I want to stop...for them," he insisted, pointing to his son and mentioning his second young one at home. He went on to explain that he had a "fool-proof plan for recovery." Every night he would ask his wife to come out to their garage at 10 p.m. and watch him blow into one of those locks people put on their car—an alcohol sensor that prevents the car from starting if the driver has been drinking. I just looked at him, and looked at that device that's supposed to stop a person from drinking.

"Danny, you don't have to re-invent the wheel," I said finally. "Hundreds of thousands people get sober by attending AA and following the Twelve Steps. Remember, we have three meetings a day here in our town."

Danny got teary. "I'm so glad I ran into you," he said.

**Twelve Steps reprinted for adaptation by permission of AA World Services, Inc. Reprinted from the Little White Booklet, Narcotics Anonymous. © 1986 by Narcotics Anonymous World Services, Inc., PO Box 9999, Van Nuys, CA 91409 ISBN 0-912075-65-1 10/00

So did he go to the meetings and engage in the process of following the Twelve Steps? Was this really his epiphany? Well, as addicts like us know, the proof is in the action. When I didn't hear of any active follow-up on Danny's part, I couldn't help wondering if he still believed that he could make it some other way, with some "thing" that was going to stop him.

Don't make the same mistake. Yes, there are many other aids to recovery, including proven treatment centers and therapists who understand addiction and recovery. But from my experience of 28 years of recovery and treating addicts of all stripes at all stages of addiction and recovery, I have come to firmly believe that at the root of every effective approach is making an investment in the Twelve Steps. You can choose to make that investment at any time.

In Section 2: "Doing the Work," I will provide pointers on how to approach some of the steps that many addicts find especially challenging. You also may want to consult my own summaries of each step that I have posted on my website: www.docdawn.com. The Twelve Step recovery community also offers many useful aides and guides to help you understand and practice the Twelve Steps.

As you will hear me emphasize again and again in this book, it's absolutely critical that you take full advantage of the support and guidance that will always be there for you via the Twelve Steps of AA, NA, and their related recovery programs. Work the steps. Go to meetings. Listen. Learn. Commit.

Now, before we continue, here's a word of caution: Some of you may already be familiar with the next few lessons in Phase I Recovery. But, don't pass too quickly over them. Recovery has much to do with repeating the same lessons over and over again. And if what we discuss is new to you, or to your loved one, I invite you to squeeze out every last drop of awareness, insight, and direction.

Lesson #2
REMEMBER—SOMETIMES THE SICKEST GET THE "WELLEST"

If you have recently hit your rock bottom and begun to clear your head from all the alcohol and drugs, you might find yourself looking at the train wreck of your out-of-control life and muttering to yourself something like, "Man, I was really sick." You may wonder how you can ever rebuild an existence that even registers close to the "normal" end of the scale, never mind something healthy and strong. The possibility of thriving in recovery may seem pretty far-fetched when you're wondering how the heck you're even going to survive out there in a life free of drugs.

Please understand that such doubts are part of the Phase I Recovery territory. The damage you have caused is real. But you know what? The possibilities for physical, emotional, and spiritual health and well-being are real too. There absolutely is hope for today and for tomorrow. In fact, a large number of addicts who follow a committed path to Phase I Recovery often make a startling discovery. I describe the "aha" this way:

Sometimes the sickest get the "wellest."

It's really true. Those who have suffered the most pain often wind up experiencing the greatest peace. Those who have done the most harm turn to doing the most good. Those who have made the worst choices begin making the best choices. I will even go so far as to suggest that you may come to develop a deep sense of gratitude for all the horrible stuff you somehow survived. It has actually opened the doorway for you to fashion a life that looks and feels completely different.

So remember that, even if you don't believe me right now, okay? There is hope for what will emerge on the other side. But for now, if you happen to be right on the cusp of choosing to invest in recovery, I am going to continue to meet you right where you are. To help that cause, I'm going to show you the tape of what I looked and sounded like when I was just beginning my own recovery.

In the Introduction I mentioned that the seed for my recovery was firmly and indelibly planted by my meeting Dr. Blair Carlson, the physician who opened my eyes with his presentation on addiction for other doctors and then held my tears while I spilled the beans on my messed up addicted life. But, as you may remember, it took me five more months before finally stopping the flood of drugs I had been pouring into my body. During that period, I was still either snorting or free-basing cocaine at home, still a threat to blow up the whole house with my preschool children in it. But I was trying to grasp that line (no pun intended) of hope, instead of one more line of white powder, that had been cast out to me. Blair had put me in touch with other physicians in recovery, including "Doctor Joe," whose words stuck with me: "Don't worry, Dawn, you don't have to figure out if you are an addict. If you are, things will get worse. Call me when they do." At first, I could not comprehend this prediction. I had seen the light. I was trying to cut down. I knew more. And yet I was still hooked. I remember calling Doctor Joe one day when I noticed that the mess of my life really wasn't getting much cleaner, and I was even more worried about what could happen.

"Oh," he said as he picked up the phone, "are things getting worse?" Well, uh, now that you mention it...

Here's the scene of the day it finally came to a head. I was getting my drugs those days from my friend Sally, the wife of a violinist who had become my cocaine dealer and mother of children about the same age as my daughters Brie and Kara. She called me and urged, "Let's get the kids together," which was code for us moms getting loaded. Usually I would have jumped at her offer, but one of the voices in my head that day was saying, "Just have one drug-free day, and see what it's like." So I declined Sally's invitation for a get-together, and she suggested instead that Kara come over and play with her daughter. I agreed to that plan and we met at a midway point. Of course, I should point out that I had already taken one black beauty (a long-acting amphetamine). Not exactly the textbook definition of staying clean for the day, I know, but progress for me.

When we met, and Sally volunteered to put Kara in her seat belt in the back seat of her car (this was before car seat days) for me, I just didn't have the adult capacity to say no, that I would prefer to do it. I trusted Sally to pack up my daughter and take her away, not even thinking that she most likely would be free-basing cocaine when she got the kids home. With light snow in the air, the snowflakes and thoughts of cocaine were all muddled in my brain. But I had one clear insight: I just gave my kid to my drug dealer. Sally could blow up the house. I was not able to follow that thought with "I have to stop right now and go get my daughter."

I went to my car, where my fingers were soon fiddling with the glove compartment lid. When it popped open, I was staring at the AA meeting list that Blair had given me months earlier. And without knowing exactly what I would do, I began driving toward the AA meeting, almost an hour away and scheduled to begin in one hour…hmmm…timing? Coincidence? God? The AA meeting site that day was in a Denver strip mall, but when I arrived where it should have been, all I could find were a fish store and a post office. I asked in the post office where to find the AA meeting, and the clerk pointed to a rusty iron staircase in the alley behind the mall. I walked up the steps and opened the door at the top. As I peered inside the smoky room, I could see maybe a dozen people there. "Come in," one of the tough-looking guys said gently. "You're in the right place." As I walked toward the seats, I realized there was only one other woman there. Still, I had this sense, which felt strange and right at the same time, that these were people with whom I could feel comfortable.

A tattooed biker handed me a copy of the book Living Sober, which I accepted with a nod before bursting into tears. But I stayed. And I listened. The lady put a cup of coffee in front of me. People were kind and friendly. They had decided, for my benefit, to focus on Step One of the Twelve Steps. As they told their stories of when they recognized that they had become powerless over their addiction and that their lives were unmanageable, I kept nodding. "You mean this is how everybody is—like me?" I said to myself. What I also kept hearing over and over was this message: Alcoholism was MY disease. It didn't matter how I got it or where it came from. I couldn't blame my parents any longer.

When I picked up Kara, I gave her an extra hug—she was safe. I did drink for a few more days, but at least when I placed my drinking glass down I placed it on top of the thick AA book. Reading about recovery and drinking alcohol at the same time! (Many months later, someone pointed out to me that I may have been unconsciously detoxing myself, reducing the amount of alcohol and pills that I consumed by a little bit each day for that first week. Or maybe this was a God thing...the God I did not yet believe in.) That was at least the beginning of a commitment to the program! When I finally stopped, my husband wanted to celebrate — and poured some sparkling cider. Realizing later that this beverage contained some alcohol, I pushed back my "official" recovery date a few days to be rigidly honest: March 9, 1984.

I began throwing the alcohol out of the house and flushing my pills down the toilet. Boy, those were some amazing multi-colored flushes! Then I had to dismantle the eight-foot high marijuana plants I had been growing outside and still had drying in my basement from the fall harvest. I shook my head as I flashed to all the time and trouble that I invested in building a fence high and sturdy enough to keep the elk out of my crop.

Was life a bundle of laughs those first few weeks? Are you kidding, with no alcohol and drugs to deal with my daily doses of anger, frustration, and anxiety? I was an irritable mess—most of the time. Then I would also have those moments of floating on a pink cloud. "This is going to be easy," I would predict. And five minutes later it would be, "I am never going to get through this alive." Does this sound familiar?

I still worried about everything, and when the regular concerns mounted up I would flash to images of ending it permanently. Suicide was my default strategy. I remember barely getting through one crazy but clean weekend and finding myself in my office on Monday morning just not seeing how I could get through the week. So I called Blair.

"Wait a minute," he said after listening for only a few seconds, "I need to check my calendar…Oh, right. It's Monday! You know, if I felt like I do on Monday on every other day of the week I'd want to end it too. But guess what—tomorrow's Tuesday."

He knew just what I needed to hear. Later, when I was approaching another meltdown while making final preparations for a trip with my kids back East, where I would see my still actively drinking parents, I called Blair again. I explained how I couldn't hold it together to get the kids packed, arrange coverage for my patients, and get everything else lined up to get away. "Oh Dawn," he sighed. "You're trying to do everything perfectly. You can't. You're just a human being and you'll never do it all perfectly. Just do it adequately and give yourself a break." Hmmm.

I took the trip, and I made it a priority to get to some recovery meetings. I also followed Blair's advice to keep the trip short and returned to the safety of my home and my regular meetings after a few days.

A short time later I took another trip east to visit family in North Carolina. The most memorable moment of this visit came during some quiet time with my 70-ish cousin Cathy, whom I had always admired and trusted. I had not told her, or my parents, that I had begun recovery from addiction. But she was studying me closely and finally said, "Dawn, you look really depressed. What's wrong?" What I was able to confide in her was that I was struggling with what I would do about my marriage, which I could see was on unstable ground.

"You know, Dawn, there's an organization known as Adult Children of Alcoholics," explained Cathy, who knew all about my parents' addiction. "With what you went through growing up, you might find it helpful." When I asked her how she knew about that, she replied, "I'm in recovery from alcoholism myself. Everyone in the family knows." Well, I didn't know. I thought for a moment and looked Cathy in the eyes.

"I'm Dawn," I said, "and I'm an alcoholic."

Cathy smiled and said, "Well, thank God."

31

She knew in that moment that, like her, I had the potential to transform from the sickest to the "wellest".

You have that potential too. It doesn't matter how big of a mess you made to get there. It doesn't matter how many times you thought about, or even tried recovery before. It doesn't matter what got you to the starting gate of recovery now. The whole picture can change—if you do what hundreds of thousands of other people like you have done and commit to a plan for recovery.

Lesson #3
BELIEVE THIS: YOU ARE *NOT* A LOSER!

"I'm such a loser!" Josh moaned to me recently. A 21-year-old soon to be college graduate, Josh wants to become a doctor. He's smart and capable, and his mother, an attorney, fully supports him in his goals. But he's got a little problem that could smash his goal into a thousand pieces. Josh is a drug addict and he has been unable to stick with a recovery program.

I saw him once as a patient, and he reluctantly acknowledged that he was hooked on OxyContin. He agreed to have me take him to an NA meeting. That was a start. But Josh admitted to me that he was resistant to the idea of any kind of God. That was a stumbling block for Danny also, as it is initially for many addicts seeking recovery, something I will discuss later. He also proclaimed, "I don't need those meetings to quit." That was a major roadblock. I told him that his thinking was misguided and not likely to lead to success, and to his mother I said, "If he really does nothing to support his recovery, I can guarantee you that he will get worse." Sure enough, he relapsed.

So Josh and I had an hour-long phone consultation, and he admitted that his fears had surged. He explained that he still really wanted to go to medical school and didn't want any reference to treatment for his addiction on his record. He had attended one or two more recovery meetings, and once he had even briefly spoken up. But he still struggled to commit to going more regularly.

"So what's really holding you back?" I asked.

"Well," he said slowly, "when I'm driving to a meeting I keep saying to myself, you are such a loser. Why do you have to go to these meetings?' And then I turn around and go home."

"Do you like music?" I asked.

"Sure, all kinds of music."

"Ever hear of Eric Clapton?"

"Come on, sure I have."

"Did you know that Eric Clapton is a recovering addict?"

I heard a pause on the phone. Something had clicked, and it wasn't the other end of the receiver. It was in Josh's brain.

In my mind, I flashed to an image of the day I met a celebrity in recovery. Before she had founded her own treatment center, Betty Ford had come to work on her recovery in Vail, Colorado. Betty's doctor happened to know Mary, my sponsor, and asked her to gather a group of women in recovery for Betty to meet. Mary had told Betty about me, and how I had gone on to become a competitive triathlete. One day, after competing in an athletic event near Vail, sitting on a bench sipping a sports drink with my husband Erik, and I spotted Betty and Gerald Ford walking toward their chauffeured limousine, their security detail in tow.

"Oh, I've got to say hello to Betty!" I shouted. I bounced up from my seat, bolted past the Secret Service agents who were watching my every move, and pulled up to Betty as she stood beside the car, about to get in. "Betty, I'm Mary's friend," I gushed. She was gracious enough to share a brief hug and a few moments of small talk. After saying goodbye, I realized I had been just a few feet from a former president of the United States and had not even said hello to him. Thankfully the Secret Service agents relaxed and did not shoot or arrest me.

No, Betty Ford was not a loser. Neither were Eric Clapton or Bonnie Raitt or Anthony Hopkins or Steven Tyler and the entire Aerosmith band or any of the other many celebrities who have embraced recovery. Ordinary folks like you and me who stop our active addiction are not losers, either. We are human beings with a disease and the tremendous courage to do something about it. And to stick with it! In your moments of doubt when negative images of yourself creep up on you like thieves in the night, remember that.

Lesson #4
IF YOU WANT TO STEER CLEAR OF RELAPSES, LEARN WHY THEY HAPPEN

If you're going to prevail in Phase I Recovery and eventually open to the possibilities of life in Phase II Recovery, you will need to deal consistently with the realities of relapse. No one who has suffered through years of addiction wants to relapse after turning to recovery. But relapses happen. Frequently. Sometimes more than once to the same person in recovery. Sometimes even when an addict has been at least making an effort, perhaps intermittently, to follow the Twelve Steps. That person may not have learned the saying common in recovery that "trying is lying."

As Yoda spoke, there is no try, just do or do not. This is all part of the reality that any of us who seeks to break the chain needs to understand. I regularly treat patients who have relapsed. Sometimes the relapse ends with…the loss of life.

Many worried addicts and their families ask me about their chances of recovery. What are the odds he or she will make it? The answer, of course, is pretty elusive. Years ago those in AA would say that well over half of those alcoholics who came to AA would stick with recovery. Is it any better today? Is it worse? What about the relapse rates for addiction to drugs other than alcohol—are they always much worse than for pure alcoholism? When it comes to cocaine and meth addicts, we think that only a small percentage, possibly as low as 10 per cent, find and sustain recovery. It appears that odds are better for heroin and other narcotic addicts, as they are for alcoholics. Did I mention that I am a recovering cocaine addict? If I can do it, so can you. For me, the odds of long-term recovery, at least 28 years, are 100 per cent, not 10 per cent.

As an MD Addictionist, I can assure you that no matter how long and to what degree you were addicted to drugs (alcohol being one such drug), you absolutely can recover. And it's entirely possible you may relapse too. The best you can do is to do everything you possibly can to try to beat those odds. And, after committing to a recovery program, the first way to do that is to gain a clearer understanding of why addicts relapse and, more importantly, what to do to avoid relapse.

I could suggest many factors for the high percentage of those who relapse, but for this lesson I'm going to focus on what I see as one the biggest: fear. It's funny, isn't it? Our fears, and our desire to cover them up, are so often a primary catalyst in leading us to drink and drug in the first place. In fact, if you look beyond the anger that so often seems to define the behavior of any addict, you'll likely find a whole lot of fear: fear of losing something or someone of value; fear of being judged or rejected; fear of not being able to control the future.

Then, when we somehow manage to stop using, at least for a while, our fears frequently are at play in prompting us to go back to the booze and pills. Why? Because when we take away our cover (drugs), the fears are still there. Only they become bigger and uglier in our mind. We can no longer deny that our particular fears aren't real, or that important. And when those fears in one way or another can be boiled down to the all-encompassing fear of not being "good enough" that so many of us had ingrained in childhood, we are especially unprepared to combat them. Deal with our fears, in a clean state? No course in school ever prepared us for that. And learning how to do it from others? Right! My parents sure could never do it, and I bet yours couldn't either.

So even in recovery we cover that fear with anger, as we did when we were using, and lash out at the family member or other undeserving person in front of us. We isolate ourselves, which only makes the fears escalate. We hear the messages: What if he does this or thinks that, or doesn't do or think that? What if I can't make enough money, can't look good enough, can't pass the test, and can't keep the girlfriend? I'm sure you have your own variation of those fear voices that tend to escalate during the roller coaster of early recovery. Know what one of mine sounded like in that crazy time? "I can't possibly stay clean. I have two children in my life!" I blurted that out at a Twelve

Step meeting in my first days in recovery, not realizing that another parent was there with her 12-year-old daughter. Kim had been clean for several years despite having a daughter in her life: Exhibit A!

Another nasty part of the fear cycle in recovery is that fears you never knew you had come ratcheting up to the surface. Your addiction had been at least somewhat successful in holding them at bay, but now they're roaring over the breaker wall. How do you keep yourself from drowning? First, admit they are there. Your fear exists — it's real to you. One way or another it's going to demand your attention, and you must take the responsibility to address it. As Dr. Joe once told me, "go ahead and have your fears, just don't let them paralyze you." The good news is that the Twelve Steps can be especially helpful in this cause, as they often are. Two that are especially critical are Step 2: came to believe that a power greater than ourselves could restore us to sanity; and Step 3: made a decision to turn our will and our lives over to the care of God as we understood Him.

As many addicts who enter recovery without a significant religious or spiritual foundation say, "What? You mean the G word?" Yes, the Twelve Steps do refer often to God. As we go along, you will hear me reference God in many contexts. When we get to the lesson "Assign a Concept of God You Can Believe In," I'll guide you on ways to deal with the God question within the cause of recovery, no matter what your views on God may happen to be. For now, let's stick with what you can concretely declare: —you are only human, not all powerful, and you need help. You may especially need help in dealing with all these deep-seated fears.

You can do your part, behaving in the most responsible way you can. Maybe you can practice using qualities such as kindness and joy, which often can serve as effective antidotes to fear. You can attend meetings and speak to your fears, or just listen to others give voice to their own anxiety and insecurities. You can talk to others who may understand and support you, and perhaps, with help as needed from a trusted therapist, begin to track the roots of all those fears. And yes, you might at least consider the possibility that you have another ally. The idea of turning over our fears to our own concept of God can be very powerful.

The more you attend meetings and get to know other addicts in recovery, the more you will learn about the triggers for relapse, along with some tips on how to recognize and deal with them. You don't need to live in fear of a relapse lurking around every corner, but you do want to enhance your awareness of what you're doing, thinking, and feeling, and how to direct your energies to the choices that will sustain your recovery. This issue of relapsing is so critical to finding your way out of addiction and building a sturdy Phase I Recovery that I am going to devote the next lesson to it as well.

Lesson #5
JUST BECAUSE YOU FEEL THE NEED TO RELAPSE DOESN'T MEAN YOU HAVE TO DO IT!

"Did you ever have a relapse?" That question was often asked me through many years of recovery. I would always answer honestly, "No, I've been clean since my first day of recovery." Yet, as I continued meeting more healthy recovering addicts almost every day, learning more about addiction and recovery and becoming increasingly committed, I came to realize that this simple explanation did not tell the whole story. So I added a further note: "Well, I may have found it necessary to relapse at times, but I've never done it."

How can that be? Like most addicts early in recovery, I did encounter triggers. I came face to face with many of the same kinds of people and situations that used to drive me to drink or drug, along with a whole bunch of new potential triggers: the deaths of both my parents only months apart; my divorce; the suicide of a close friend just before her 40th birthday and not long before I would turn 40; assorted conflicts with my daughters as they grew into adolescents, and many more events that stabbed me with grief or pain. Sometimes that pain felt so horrible that I didn't believe I could bear it.

In a way, those experiences seemed to be telling me that I needed those old reliable methods of covering the pain. Some urge was insisting that I had to have those drugs again. Yet, on some semi-conscious level, I knew they would not help for more than a few minutes or hours. The saying, "recovery messes up your drinking and using," really applied to me. I may have wanted relief, may have thought about drugs, and imagined how they could cover the agony like they used to, but I just didn't reach for them.

Most of all, as someone who had survived two active suicide attempts and had danced with the plan for a third and most likely fatal try, I was just grateful to be alive. That gratitude often trumped the

39

nagging trigger to relapse. I also came to see that those triggering events were just part of reality. Using wasn't going to make things any better. What could and would make it better was talking to people in my recovery community and going to meetings. As we say, sharing cuts the pain in half and doubles the pleasure.

I also did something else that I suggest that you do if you are in that vulnerable period of Phase I Recovery and desperately want to avoid a relapse. I kept all the alcohol and drugs out of my house, and I did not spend time around people who were using. If I ever felt overwhelmed by the need to relapse, I would have to go out of my way to do it. When I even began to think about cocaine, my drug of choice, had I been around people who were using it, I just might have inched closer to the path I sought so hard to stay off. I remember when I was separating from my husband and moving my belongings to my new home, I opened a desk drawer and stumbled upon a gram of cocaine I had missed on my previous clean sweeps. "Ah, poison!" I shouted to myself. I snatched it up, raced to the toilet, and flushed it—a "snow seal." After high-fiving myself in the mirror, I promptly called my sponsor, another woman who had helped me through the steps, and got myself to a meeting that night.

So don't be caught off guard when you experience those moments of temptation and need. Have a plan, phone numbers ready to use, meetings available at all times, a God to call on when no one else answers, whatever you need. Don't do drugs, no matter what, no matter what! This is part of the new territory. Life in early recovery is no picnic. But reach instead for the tools and resources to stay clean, stay on the path of Phase I Recovery. You can do it.

When you are able to conquer those moments when you feel the temptation to relapse, side-stepping any trigger that could derail your recovery journey, make sure you celebrate that triumph too. It will help you create the same result the next time.

Now there's one more twist to this picture of the urge to use again I'd like to unravel: the seeds of a relapse may be planted long before the actual slip. A long-time patient recently called me from New York. At age 67, Kathleen certainly doesn't look like an addict. She's educated, wealthy and articulate—a vivid example of how appearances can be deceiving. Kathleen happens to be addicted to prescription pain-killers, a dramatic and dangerous trend we'll discuss in more detail in Part 2 in our exploration into the role of healthcare professionals in addiction and recovery. She called me because she had recently relapsed, and when she explained the particulars I was struck by her reference to the starting point for falling into her old habit.

"It really began two years ago," she said. "I had been off the prescription narcotics for some time and was enjoying a vacation with friends in Ireland. They invited me to have a little Irish beer with them, and I wound up accepting their invitation. I remember my exact thoughts at the time: I've refrained from using the drugs. I'm just here to enjoy myself. I deserve this!"

I wasn't surprised by what happened next. While Kathleen did not suddenly begin drinking regularly, and she did not immediately reach for the pain pills when she got home from Ireland, a seed had been planted. Two years later she did resume regularly abusing prescription drugs, and she knew that this relapse could be traced directly to that moment of doing something she "deserved" two years earlier.

Kathleen had fallen into the "entitlement mindset." Have you ever experienced it? You would know by finding yourself saying things like, "I've worked my butt off all day. I deserve a little drink" or "I've stayed off the booze for three weeks. I can have a few hits of marijuana because I deserve a little treat." Entitlement runs along the same continuum that shows up as victimhood at the other end: "No one else has to deal with all these problems all day long. I've got to find some relief." It's all part of the voice of denial. When you listen to those voices, your brain is setting you up for failure, even if it takes a while for the failure to manifest itself. When you, like Kathleen, combine a lingering desire to use alcohol or any drug with the thought that you deserve it, you have planted the seed. And that seed, left unattended, can grow into a nasty relapse.

Something else was going on for Kathleen during those two years since the seed was planted for a relapse. She was not attending recovery meetings consistently. Nor was she diligently working the Twelve Steps. She never dealt with her resentments (Step 4), or her character defects (Step 7), or made amends (Step 9). Had she been firmly immersed in recovery, working with a sponsor and part of a home group, her odds of avoiding relapse, or coming back from one rapidly, would have been far greater.

Of course, as we just discussed, you don't have to relapse just because you feel the need or you had one potentially destructive thought. You can make different choices. Let's go back to Kathleen and that first moment of choice. She could have noticed her yearning to add to her vacation fun with a "harmless" beer and then stopped right there—halted by the recognition that allowing herself to indulge in any drug, and listening to that "I deserve this" voice, would put her on to road to a full relapse. She could have declined her friend's invitation to go along with the Irish drinking crowd and summoned an alternative beverage, even making a joke of lifting her "pint of club soda" to keep in the light-hearted spirit. Or, even after missing that moment and having that Irish beer, she could have followed up with an immediate call to me or to her sponsor to talk out her experience and steer herself quickly back to her recovery program. In other words, the seed that had been planted could have been dug up before it grew from a onetime slip into a full-fledged relapse, which in Kathleen's case took the form of major consumption of those pain pills, something that was going to take a lot of time and much hard work to reverse. The disease of addiction is so serious and so advanced in her case, I feared that she might never return to recovery.

So keep a lookout for those seeds of slippage that may be popping up in your life in early recovery. If you hear those voices of entitlement, remind yourself that what you really deserve is a life free of addiction. And admit to yourself that if you inadvertently planted a seed for a potential relapse, you're going to have to go brush it aside or dig it up before it undermines your Phase I Recovery.

Lesson #6
DON'T FALL INTO OTHER ADDICTIVE PRACTICES

If you are committed to building your Phase I Recovery, you need to keep your eyes on the prize. Your goal, simply, is to be free of addiction. And yes, that includes being free of Process Addictions, or behavioral addictions: smoking, gambling, compulsive overeating, anorexia or bulimia, compulsive sexual behavior, endless texting, excessive time with TV or computers, etc.

It so happens that addicts just breaking free from their drug often call upon substitutes in a vain attempt to provide some of the same "payoffs" they gained from drinking or drugging: a temporary relief from anxiety; covering other difficult feelings; avoiding specific problems and people; feeling good enough about themselves for a brief period, etc. Essentially, before significant emotional and spiritual growth occurs, addicts are still attempting to fill the void. That emptiness is so gnawing, so painful, that we try anything to fill it. I'll have much more to say about this later. So if you haven't progressed far enough in your recovery to address those issues, you may find yourself suddenly turning to, or becoming more obsessive in your behavior in the areas of smoking, gambling, sex, over-eating or under-eating, work, TV, etc. Whether you know it or not, you are calling upon those practices in the continuing service of covering or changing feelings, providing a brief high, or seeking to deny your emotional and spiritual pain and emptiness. It's like the alcoholic who switches to just beer and wine when he believes that vodka caused the problems, failing to see that he, not the alcohol, and certainly not the type of alcohol, is the problem. For the addict, it is what he does with drugs and what they do to him that is the problem: "Wherever he goes, there he is!" Just switching drinks or bars will not help.

It's the same with increasing frequency of over-eating, or having excessive, inappropriate, often destructive sex, or gambling, thinking that it's "better" than the addiction that caused the real problem. So repeat after me: "It is the addict, not the substance or process that is the problem." That means you must face the reality that the answers to what you are seeking in life are not to be found in some practice you become addicted to. And please, spare me the same old lines of denial about your level of involvement in these Process Addictions that you used to spew out for your primary addiction: "I don't do it that much, I only do it on the weekends, etc." Denial is still denial. The answers to what you are after can only be found in recovery, in being free of addiction. The good news regarding being hooked on a practice is that you can find recovery groups for many of those Process Addictions, just as you can for alcohol or drug addiction. For example, you may recognize the need to seek out Gamblers Anonymous, Overeaters Anonymous or Sex Addicts Anonymous.

So do not get caught in the trap of thinking that you have turned the corner by ceasing one addiction while loading up one or more other addictions. Stay with your recovery program. Be honest with yourself and others about those Process Addictions. Cultivate a relationship with your Higher Power. Bring more healthy people and healthy influences into your life. You will find that even with this part of the journey—getting free of all addictions—you are not alone.

Lesson #7
BEWARE OF THOSE AROUND YOU STUCK IN THEIR DENIAL

I remember vividly my mother's response when I first informed her that I had entered recovery and was regularly attending Twelve Step meetings. "Oh, you're doing this for your patients, right?" She could grasp that I was assisting patients in recovery in my practice, but the idea that her own daughter was admitting to her addiction and seeking help for it just did not compute. Then, after I had invited her to look at the AA Big Book herself, she quipped, "Oh, so now you're getting a course in religion?" Remember, she was the daughter of a Southern Baptist minister. I guess when she saw the references to God in the Twelve Steps, she jumped to something known, familiar...safer.

Though I was disappointed in her response at the time, it was certainly understandable that my mother would be in denial about the reality of my having a problem with addiction when she was an addict herself. Sadly, Mom didn't stop drinking right up until her death from colon cancer at age 76. From time to time I would urge her to attend just one AA meeting, but she would lament, "Well, those meetings are in the evening, you know. I don't want to go out then." Translation: "I usually start drinking long before the meeting time of 7 or 8 p.m."

The important lesson for me was to not allow someone else's denial of my addiction, or their own, to become an active voice in my own mind. That would have been one big swerve off the road to recovery. So during your recovery, make sure you protect yourself from being swayed or pulled into doubt about the importance of what you have chosen and seek to continue doing by others who do not understand or believe you have the need to do so. My original sponsor, Linda told me that I may have to "defend" my alcoholism someday...others would not get it that I needed to be drug and alcohol free. Other addicts still actively using are the most likely sources of such doubting comments. That's one good reason you should no longer hang out with addicts you know. But, because recovery programs tend to operate in the shadows of everyday life, even well-meaning non-addicts sometimes join the denial chorus.

I remember the first time I visited my now ex-husbands' parents in Baltimore after I had begun my recovery. He didn't want his parents to know that I was not drinking. In other words, he wanted to deny in their presence that I had ever had a problem with alcohol and drugs in the first place. While I certainly didn't agree with his line of thinking—okay, I thought it was crazy—I complied when we first arrived. But, I was so anxious about trying to keep up the facade, I couldn't sleep. The next evening at dinner, my mother-in-law kept offering me alcohol, really pushing the wine with our meal. I kept declining. Noting that her looks were growing more and more puzzled, I finally blurted out, "I have a problem with alcohol. I've stopped drinking. My parents are both alcoholics too."

"No, they can't be!" she retorted. "Your mom goes swimming. I see her. She looks fine. She can't have a problem."

Does this response from others sound familiar? Do you hear the voice of denial not only from your drinking buddies but also from family members who think they know everything about you and simply can't wrap their minds around this idea that you are an addict? If so, I understand your frustration. Sometimes the denial even comes from the spouse who had been urging their loved one to seek recovery but stumbles into a moment of doubt over whether they have "done the right thing" when they see the breadth and depth of the changes that will be required in both their lives.

Your job is very simple: do not let their denial become your denial. You are doing the right thing, and the more committed you become to Phase I Recovery, the more others around you will not only accept the reality but embrace it with you. In the meantime, spend more time around the courageous men and women who attend meetings and who have devoted themselves to their recovery. I'm sure they'll have something to say about that denial you're getting from others around you!

Lesson #8
YOUR MIND IS LIKE A RIVER,
SO YOU'VE GOT TO
CHANGE THE FLOW

When we consider how the brain of an addict functions, we can make a natural comparison to a fast-moving river. Bear with me for just a moment as I put on my M.D. Addictionist hat and walk us through the medical terrain to show you how this works and, more important, how it can help you avoid relapse and stay on the path of Phase I Recovery.

The longer a swift river stays in its groove in the ground, the more difficult it is to change course. After all, that river has been flowing down the same route for years, decades, or centuries. The human brain does the same thing. The neurochemical pathways in our brains are set in motion by the input we get before birth when our brain just begins to form. Electrical impulses develop and chemicals such as dopamine, epinephrine, serotonin, and endorphins appear and begin to do their work. These chemicals establish routes in our brains, influenced by all the input we receive in our life. Much of the way we think, feel, and behave is established by the pathway formed from the reaction of these chemicals to the world around us: parents, teachers, friends—everything that happens to us. That river that is our mind is flowing, the chemicals and electrical impulses finding their pathway. Each day the specific pathway gets bigger and stronger, like the river that accumulates more force as it flows. And like the river, it gets harder and harder to change course.

So what happens when you're an addict and practically every life situation calls for using drugs? That ingrained neurochemical pathway began whenever you started using alcohol or substances to cover up your pain, sadness, low self-esteem, or emptiness so you could temporarily feel good, or at least okay. You reinforced that pathway by regular use of drugs. The river that said "use drugs" was

47

rushing down the mountain fast and furious and did not want to be stopped. If you wanted to cease using drugs, you had to somehow find a way to alter the reflex, to change the flow of the river or neurochemical pathway. So do you know what you actually did to begin your recovery? You began to dam up the river!

Like beaver dams in real rivers, you started to build a dam in your brain. The first task was to tap the strength and courage to refuse to use for just one day, and then another day, and then a third day. You've done that. But your "beaver" mission does not end there. You've still got lots more work to do. Specifically, you still have to deal with your brain. That river has not yet stopped flowing, and there's a powerful pathway that knows nothing except how to use drugs. You helped by laying a log across part of the river by not using anything mind altering. Now you've got to keep piling more logs on top to make the barrier stronger. That's really what you're doing by going to recovery meetings, working the Twelve Steps, and sticking with all the other parts of your Phase I Recovery program. You are gradually stopping the flow of water in the river with each thought and behavior that is different from what you have done millions of times in the past. You are changing the neurochemistry in your brain. Pretty powerful!

As you strengthen your recovery, the flow of water in the river and of chemicals in your brain will have to find another route. Rivers form rivulets, little streams off the main river, if the main flow is blocked. The vascular system in the human body does the same: blocks off one route, such as a gradually forming plaque or clot in a blood vessel, and sometimes your body will form others, collateral vessels to bypass the blocked one. Your brain follows a similar process. It will form new pathways, new reflexes, when you refuse to allow the old ones to continue. The thoughts and behaviors have to go somewhere...when they cannot do the same old thing, they change. Soon the new pathway is available to you—you strengthen your reflex to say, "no thank you" when offered your old drug of choice. Your thinking is changing; your behavior is changing.

Yet, as any good beaver knows, dams demand almost constant attention. Beavers don't work alone, either. Their friends and family are right there helping. That new rivulet at first is tiny, with just a small stream of water going through it. That's why you've got to get more logs, to form a more complete barrier to the water or, in other words, to stop the chemical pathway that tells you to use drugs. So grow the new way. Feed the "not in active addiction" information to your brain. And give your friends something to talk about when they ask you what's new and you say, "Oh, just looking for a few new logs to pile on my dam."

Before we leave the subject of brain chemistry, bear with me while I add one more idea of how you can impact what's going on in your whole neurochemical system. Recovering addicts have a saying: "We cannot always think our way into right acting, but we can act our way into right thinking." Or, more simply, "fake it 'til you make it." Let's explore how that works.

When we do something positive, it changes how we feel. Volunteering to do something to help others—things like baking cookies for a friend, shoveling snow for a neighbor, pitching in at the Salvation Army or community food bank, packing Christmas baskets at a church, or visiting a retirement home and reading to a woman who has lost her eyesight—just makes you feel good. And feeling good, without getting high on drugs, is something you want to do more and more to sustain your recovery.

Here's where it gets interesting. Your brain chemistry changes with different activities and behavior. We train our brain to function in a certain way, promoting the flow of neurochemicals and electrical connections (remember the river!) in either positive or negative directions, reacting and responding in the way it always has...until we change. So when we do nice things—even something as simple as smiling, saying kind words, or holding a door open for someone—our brain chemistry changes for the better. We start a cycle in our brain of feeling good and seeking more ways to change our behavior to feed on that positive response. You make the decision to do something helpful, you feel better, you have more energy to do something else nice, then you feel even better, and so on. It's an upward spiral.

There's more. When you begin to feel good a little more often, you also can make the choice to express gratitude for this change in your life. You can practice expressing it every day, in new and different ways. When you were using and would complain about something, that

49

whining became a downward spiral around the drain pipe and on to hatred of self and isolation from others. Now you can shift to an upward spiral by focusing on gratitude.

So find gratitude for something in your life, even if you have to start by "pretending" to be grateful. Look around your life in recovery and start a gratitude list. If nothing else, you can begin with having enough food to eat or not being terminally ill, or not being caught in the aftermath of a hurricane or earthquake. Then take inventory of those good feelings you have been experiencing with your acts of kindness and other positive acts. And, what about gratitude for just having the opportunity to be in recovery? After everything you went through while using drugs, is there any other greater gift that you could receive in your life?

Starting today, you can wake up every morning and find something positive to do, and something real to feel grateful for. This is a choice. Maybe that choice was not readily available to you before you stopped using drugs, but it's here now. Reach out and grab it, and each day you do, you will find the pull to keep repeating this new behavior getting stronger and stronger. As Abraham Lincoln once said, "Most people are about as happy as they make up their minds to be."

Lesson #9
WHEN YOUR FACADE CRUMBLES, REAL DISCOVERY BEGINS

Have you ever read Scott Peck's The Road Less Traveled? If not, I recommend it. It begins with one of those classic opening lines: "Life is difficult." Sounds like a real downer for an inspirational book, doesn't it? It's really just the opposite. He goes on to say that once we accept that reality, life actually gets easier. More acceptable. Full of possibilities even. This is an important piece of basic awareness that most addicts fail to grasp. They cling to the notion that their life is difficult—more like impossible—and they believe they need to find something to cover it up, keep a lid on it, make it all go away, if even for a few hours. So they adopt a facade.

As addicts, we are convinced that drugs will make us feel better, lift us out of the pits, and at least elevate us to that place of being "okay." Instead, we discover that addiction robs us of ourselves, stealing our relationships with family and friends, our self-respect, and our peace and joy. On the surface we may look happy, the life-of-the-party addicts, but inside we harbor deep pain. We may build seemingly productive and successful lives, while seething with anger and resentment that often spill out around those who care about us. Also, though we may not consciously realize it, we are not only angry but scared, hurt, and sad.

As the years go by, and our addiction controls us more and more, we keep trying harder to get what we think we want, what we believe will make us feel good. Those fears of losing something we have or not getting something we want keep coming up. We keep doing, using, and blurring our feelings with our chosen substance. We're really trying desperately to maintain that façade that has become a part of us.

Then look what happens when we begin embracing recovery. That mask just doesn't work anymore. Doesn't fit. Can't boot up. Just crumbles into a pile of dust, leaving us to face everything we were determined to deny or push aside.

Is that crumbling of the façade scary or disorienting in the early recovery phase? You bet it is. As an addict in the vulnerable time of Phase I Recovery, you may find yourself feeling much more irritable or discontented. You may be experiencing what's sometimes called the "empty self." People early in recovery often describe it as the wind blowing through them. Does that sound like the, "life is difficult" line from Scott Peck's book? Again, it can be a catalyst for drastic change. Becoming aware of your discontent, really knowing it, can be the first step toward what ultimately may grow into a deep inner peace. You learn more of who you really are, under your mask. You gain a greater understanding of what really matters to you. Many of us have several masks: work, son or daughter, parent, student and more; recovery allows us to integrate all of the above and become our true self, just one of us, not hiding from anyone. I remember when I decided that I could no longer keep secrets. At about 6 months of sobriety, I became willing to tell anyone, when appropriate, that I was in recovery, and tell my recovery community what I did for a living. No one was especially shocked at me "coming out" and I got to stop worrying that someone would find out and begin just being me.

That's not an easy process, of course. Bummer. It seems like very little of the work of Phase I Recovery is easy, right? Perhaps it's not easy, but often very straightforward and rich with possibilities. Because when you are left with the reality of your empty self, you discover first of all that the solution is not external. This is another part of recovery where God or something spiritual can come in. Yes, I'm using the "G" word again. Wherever you happen to be on the spiritual belief spectrum, I'm going to invite you to just "pretend" with me for a moment here.

There is a question often posed in spiritual circles that goes something like this: Are we human beings having a spiritual experience or spiritual beings having a human experience? You skeptics might answer "neither," insisting that we are just human beings and that any idea about what happens before or after this life we are in now is bogus. Again, just try this on for now. What if this life on planet earth is just a blip in our being? Maybe before we came here, we were spirits—part of, yet separate from God—sent to earth for a period of time. Then we got here and got distracted by all our doings and all our stuff. We became our bodies, our behavior, our thoughts, and along the way we neglected our spirit and grew ever more separated from God. After some time existing in this separation, we began to hurt. And for many of us, we turned to addiction. And we put on our masks, our pretenses. We became human doings, not human beings.

Now what if, as part of this recovery process, we can find relief from our emptiness by returning to this idea of getting connected to God? So now, if we humble ourselves and seek God, in the spirit of the Twelve Steps, we find Him right where we left Him and happy to have us back. What if reuniting with our spiritual selves by tuning into a relationship with God turns out to be one of the keys to finding the inner peace we yearn for?

There is much more to the puzzle of finding your way out of addiction during Phase I Recovery and discovering the path to a healthy and harmonious life. But if you are intrigued by this idea of filling your void with a reunion with the spiritual self you really are, I invite you to try it on and explore it further in your own way. You may or may not be ready to accept a relationship with God, so just pry your mind open and consider it. Maybe you can just "dance" with this image of us all having been just little spirits floating around in the clouds. At least it's a more attractive and useful starting point for putting together the story behind our pretense than the one that starts with: "I'm not okay."

Does answering those "why" questions help? I don't think so. Here's a substitute Q & A: Question: "Why?" Answer: "It doesn't matter".

SECTION 2: DOING THE WORK

Lesson #10
STOP ASKING "WHY"

Addicts spend a lot of time asking why: why did that cop have to pull me over and give me a DUI? Why did my boss look at me that way? Why can't my wife stop badgering me about my drinking? Why won't my kids keep quiet when I'm feeling sick after a night of partying?

Often when addicts are seeking their way in Phase I Recovery, the whys don't stop, they just shift: Why do I have to go to these meetings all the time? Why did my parents have to give me this disease of addiction? Why can't I just be able to drink once in a while?

If you like quick, direct, simple advice, this is a lesson for you: Stop Asking Why!

There may be answers to your "why" questions, perhaps many answers, but what you need most right now is a solution. You need to find a way out of your addiction, a way to get on the recovery path and stay on it. You don't need to get caught in the illusion that if you just know why, you can create change. "Why" is the refrain of the two-year old and the teenager. Never ending and always prompting another question, not a solution, "why" becomes a mental gyration. "Why" is the booby prize. We can speculate, understand the psychodynamics, believe we know the pathway we have followed to our present state of being, or the state of self destruction that finally got us into recovery, and still continue down said pathway. Here's an illustration of how easily we addicts can get tangled in the whys:

Question: "Why did I get loaded AGAIN!?" Answer: "Because I am an addict."

Question: "Why am I an addict?" Answer: "Because I use too many drugs, or because my solution to the problem of life is in one more chemical, or because both of my parents are alcoholic, or because I had a crappy childhood."

Does answering those "why" questions help? I don't think so. Here's a substitute Q & A: Question: "Why?" Answer: "It doesn't matter".

The answer to "why" is not the solution. Did you ever learn the basic questions in school known as the five Ws and H: who, what, when, where, why, and how? Cross the "why" off the list, and work the other questions: Who can help and support me in my recovery program? What can I do differently the next time I sense one of my trigger to use drugs? When and where is the next recovery meeting? How can I continue to build on the progress I have made?

The answers to "why" will come, but much later in your recovery program, when you have gone further into your inquiry of your life's choices so far. Right now, as you dig in to do the hard work of Phase I Recovery, you need the concrete, the basics. Use your brain, now that it is no longer clouded with drugs, to make reasonable and logical decisions. Get help from someone who knows, someone who has been there. Act on your decisions. Surround yourself with people who live the way you want to live, not your old friends who still drink or use other drugs. Get more physical exercise. Cultivate the good habits that you may be slowly integrating into your life in Phase I Recovery.

If you really want a way to be different from your addictive past, keep asking those kinds of concrete questions. Follow the clues that point toward a solution. Choose a path of recovery and take it. If you get the results you are seeking—if it helps build on your recovery—stay on that pathway. If you don't like the results, choose a different pathway. Just don't waste too much time and energy on "why".

Lesson #11
To Grow Emotionally and Spiritually, You Need to Know HOW

Here's another lesson from the pragmatic toolbox of Phase I Recovery. In my work with patients in recovery, I've utilized a simple system which I first learned about in my early recovery. You can use it for further exploration on your own journey. Here's the system: to grow emotionally and spiritually in recovery, you must know HOW: Honesty; Open-mindedness; Willingness.

Honesty

Honesty, especially with ourselves, is tough! Alone in our own heads, we addicts tend to be in bad company. We are bombarded with the negative messages we have heard much of our lives, and seeking the solitude to reflect honestly on our lives seems like an invitation to further beat ourselves up. So HOW do we become honest with ourselves during recovery? It usually takes not only self-searching but also letting at least one other person—a mentor, therapist, or a trusted, responsible, and mature friend—to really get to know us. Sound scary? Sure, acknowledging our own behavior as well as our thoughts to ourselves, much less to another person, can be intimidating. We're going to get a glimpse of, and maybe let someone else see, who we really are. But the more we commit to the process and put it in motion, the more we learn that just talking to another human being about ourselves is healing. We find out there are others who understand, who have been there, who feel or have felt just like us. Other people have done some of the same embarrassing and shameful things we have done.

Honesty with ourselves and others frees us. We no longer have to worry about getting caught, about what story (lie) we told, who knows what, or anything else. We are just as sick as our secrets and if we lose the secrets, we get to heal just a little bit more.

Open-mindedness

I've often heard it said that the human mind is like a parachute: it only works when it is open. Real emotional and spiritual growth, the kind that will sustain you in Phase I Recovery, requires prying open your mind and letting in something new.

For addicts, a critical initial act of practicing open-mindedness is to listen to those who point out our signs of addiction, even if it's the 20th time they told us, or even if it's a doctor in an emergency room after an overdose. Most addicts don't believe they have a problem until a crisis occurs, usually after they have ignored signs obvious to others for years. No one I know puts on his or her high school or college graduation goal list "to become a member in good standing of AA." So, one way or another, to get to the starting point of recovery you most likely heard the messages in a different light. Your mind opened, at least a crack.

Now, in committing to do the work of Phase I Recovery, being open-minded takes on a new dimension. Almost everyone, addict or not, has formed some opinion about Twelve Step groups, usually without visiting them at all. Perhaps they went once or twice, but never considered trying to practice the new behaviors and new ways of thinking that worked for those attending. The most common criticisms I hear tend to run along these lines: "Not for me." "I can do it myself." "I don't need help." "AA is too religious for me." "Someone might see me there."

If any of those assumptions ring true for you as you seek help in recovery, you have a chance to become more open-minded. Consider pretending that you don't have any opinion about Twelve Step groups. Consider opening your mind to an organization that is responsible for millions of alcoholics and addicts getting and staying sober and clean. Many have found they could change, just by opening their minds to the experience of others and listening to another perspective. It wasn't easy for many of them to let go of their hard and fast opinions in the beginning, either.

When you become even a little more open-minded about choices that can assist you in your recovery, you also may seek out a therapist who understands addiction and can serve as another anchor in your stormy times. What's that, did you just find yourself saying, "But I tried therapy before and it didn't work for me because...?" Consider that you might have a different experience this time. First, instead of seeking out a therapist because of all the problems you are having dealing with those other people and situations in your life, this time you have the wisdom and knowledge to recognize that you are in search of help for your addiction recovery. You are ready to focus on you. That's what being open-minded is all about, and once you make that decision you will be amazed at how willing others are to help.

Willingness

The change needed to sustain and build your Phase I Recovery requires a willingness to change, to progress, to recover. But it's not enough simply to tell yourself you are willing to do the work of recovery. Willingness also means taking action. Just as "the proof of the pudding is in the tasting," so too is "the proof of the willingness is in the action." As addicts, we used to find it easier to be thinking, talking, philosophizing, or bull-------- about our drinking and drugging than to take the action to stop. Now we must back up our words about being "willing to quit" with doing what it takes to set forth on a new course of action.

But there's an even trickier part to this idea of willingness: it's not a one-time decision or action. Every bar serves alcohol to people who were willing to stop drinking—for a day, a week, a month, or even years...and started up again. In each case, the addict initially had the willingness and took the action. But then, somewhere along the way, they became unwilling and ceased taking the action to sustain the change. In other words, no recovery meetings, no therapy, no change in the company they kept, etc. And they wound up back at the bar.

Look, I know that change is tough, commitment is tougher, and immediate gratification (drinking or drugging) is, well, immediate. But guess what? Part of your newly found reality in Phase I Recovery is waking up to this truth: willingness to change often means not having all our wants immediately gratified. Well, not gratified in the old ways.

But stick with me, and keep reading these lessons. You will be learning much more about new possibilities for gratification, for fulfillment, for peace, for happiness. Just keep in mind that you will need to know HOW.

Lesson #12
TO BEGIN ACTING YOUR AGE,
TAKE COMMUNICATIONS 101

Poor me, poor me, pour me another drink. If you are an addict in Phase I Recovery, or you have a loved one whose life was driven by booze and drugs, you probably recognize that theme song. It's a common mantra of the victim, the whiner, and a classification that often fits the bill of an addict before recovery.

"Why does it always happen to me?" they moan in response to all kinds of life situations that somehow seem to track their days and nights: missing an appointment or arriving late; losing things like their cell phone, wallet, or car keys; forgetting to return calls; alienating friends and family; getting passed over for a job or promotion; getting hit with late fees and penalties for not paying credit card bills on time, etc. For an addict, this "why does it always happen to me" is an all-too-familiar refrain. Why? Simple—they haven't grown up enough to take personal responsibility. Everyone makes occasional mistakes; for the irresponsible, mistakes are a daily occurrence and a way of life.

If we began drinking and drugging as a teenager, the drugs stripped away the opportunity for the natural emotional growth and maturity that comes sometime during adolescence and early adulthood. All that time in a mind-altered state kept us from learning what those who are clean, and present, got to learn: constructive and functional ways to live, appropriate conflict resolution, how to deal with feelings, how to build healthy relationships, how to take responsibility for ourselves and not take responsibility for things that are not our job. (Note: You can learn more about this in the forthcoming book *My Job or God's Job?* by Erik Landvik). Simply put, we addicts who spent much of our time loaded never had the chance to become emotionally mature adults.

So what does that mean for addicts who have entered the vulnerable period of Phase I Recovery, when growth and maturity are vital to staying on track? It means they begin the journey stuck at the maturity level at which they happened to be before addiction took over their lives. In other words, if you as a spouse of an addict in recovery are tempted to blurt out, "Act your age," recognize that their real age, their age of maturity, may be 14 or 15, or even younger—whenever they began using drugs. They've got a lot of catching up to do.

As an addict, you need to accept this dose of reality. Do not get caught in a false sense of euphoria in which you believe that simply because you have stopped using drugs you will begin making nothing but clear, rational, mature decisions regarding the people and situations in your life. No way—not when you've got the maturity of a teenager! Here's what is different: now that your mind is no longer drug-altered, you have the opportunity to start growing up again. You do that first and foremost by focusing on just what you need to do to support your Phase I Recovery, by working the Twelve Steps and practicing the lessons we're discussing. You also can invite yourself to begin to gain awareness of all those ways that you still need to grow and change to catch up to your chronological age in important areas. Talking to friends in recovery, a sponsor, or a therapist can help you sort out these new choices and teach you more mature approaches to the stuff of everyday life.

Listen, I know this is a humbling, even baffling byproduct of choosing recovery and pushing through the first six months or first year or two. Who wants to admit they have to learn how to grow up? I had to accept the reality that, as a woman in her mid-30s in early recovery, I was still stuck at a teenage maturity level. And I was taking care of two young kids and trying to sort out a marriage in conflict at the time. Did I make wise, mature, adult decisions every time? Ha! But what I was willing to do was to fully invest my energy into my recovery program and ask, ask, ask for help for what seemed new, confusing, or overwhelming to me as an overgrown adolescent in a very adult situation. Of course, retaining playful, happy childlike ability to have fun is crucial...find a balance and don't grow up too much!

Want to know what else can help you in a big way? Now that your mind is becoming clear, and you're not completely absorbed in your old whining, poor-me mindset, take a look around at other people who have had to take on life challenges that they weren't trained to handle. Learn from your neighbor with cancer who is able to express gratitude for another day alive or the child with cerebral palsy who smiles at simply being outdoors. Pay attention to news reports of hurricane or tornado victims who lost loved ones and most of their material possessions and yet share what little they have left with friends, neighbors, and strangers in worse need than them.

They can help teach you that when you are able to let go of being the victim, you may be surprised at how naturally you will begin to make choices that will raise your own spirits, while uplifting those around you. Slowly, over time, you'll begin to behave appropriately, as an adult when required, yet keeping that childlike wonder at life itself.

If you're looking for a more tangible starting point, here's one idea to try on. As an addict in Phase I Recovery, there's a pretty good chance that you are struggling with trying to communicate with others about what you need, what you want, and what you feel. Remember, we addicts breaking the chain of addiction have just escaped from a foggy, drugged world. For years, we would misinterpret what was said to us, take things too personally, and flounder in trying to perceive a situation correctly and express ourselves in the middle of it. That inability to clearly communicate simply isn't going to change overnight.

When I entered recovery I had no language for all the many thoughts and feelings swirling around in me. It was all so new, and I was lacking in the basics of communication, never mind trying to articulate the strong emotions and raw insights bursting forth. If I had tried to sit down with a psychologist and verbalize my experience, what would come out would have been a bunch of jumbled phrases and convoluted questions. The psychologist might have made more sense out of listening to someone who had just landed from Mars!

So how can you learn to communicate in an effective, appropriate manner to support your Phase I Recovery and begin to act your age? First, get good at listening. Most addicts are so into themselves when using, they have little experience in simply listening to someone else share their experience. Going to meetings and just sitting as you absorb the stories, experiences, and reflections communicated by others in recovery will help you in three critical ways. First, you can begin to quiet your own mind chatter so that you have a more peaceful frame of reference to communicate thoughts and feelings of your own. Second, you will be hearing others expressing things that you can fully relate to; their ability to give voice to those feelings will help you find the words to communicate your experience. Third, when you move from just listening to talking to others within the safe confines of your recovery community, they will offer patience and understanding of your flustering and floundering. They've been there. When you get stuck trying to pull out the right words, they may even help you finish your sentences. They know what will fill in the blanks.

You also can enhance your communication skills in Phase I Recovery by sticking to simple facts and tangible reference points. So when you're trying to explain your experience to someone who wants to know you and can support you, tell that person how many meetings you have attended in the last week, or if you have sponsor, or if you've begun a physical activity, or if you have specific questions about recovery that the other person may be able to address.

For you doctors and therapists out there, you can support your patient in recovery in communicating more effectively by asking direct questions and steering them to answer in a clear, direct manner. Keep it simple. Keep things straight. Over time, you addicts will find increasingly more words to make sense of what's happening to you in a way that enhances your recovery efforts. This is an important acquired skill, because believe me, as you go deeper into the work of Phase I Recovery you're going to have a lot to talk about.

Lesson #13
LOOKING FOR A "SAFE" DRUG? MAKE ENDORPHINS

You know all about the unsafe drugs, and in Part II I will be discussing some you may not be aware of. Want to learn about some "safe" drugs, which you are free to use during a stable and productive Phase I Recovery? The drugs I have in mind are called endorphins, and they are the body's natural painkillers. They're also stimulants. Have you heard the expression "a runner's high?" That's a reference to the wonderful work of endorphins, and you can get them without going to the streets or to a doctor's office for a prescription. And they're free.

Physical exercise that produces endorphins can be invaluable in building your Phase I Recovery. Exercise stimulates our brain to produce its own natural chemicals, and these endorphins are something your brain is really hungry for in early recovery. Why? Addiction depletes the brain of many of its mood-stabilizing neurochemicals. The endorphins stimulated by exercise help create equilibrium in our thinking and feeling.

When you bring regular physical activity of almost any kind into your recovery, you are on your way to improving not only your physical health but your emotional and spiritual well-being too. Outdoor physical activities allow sunlight to add its own healing properties to our brains and bodies. Vigorous exercise leaves us with that wonderful exhaustion, a signal of the goal reached, the fight finished. We know we have done something positive for our bodies. Along the way, we may release anger and other emotional pain. Then we discover how feeling good about our bodies promotes feeling good about ourselves in general, making us more confident and better equipped to deal with the thoughts and feelings that could trigger a relapse. The gains from physical activity also include being more able to focus on the emotional work of recovery and to embrace the full spectrum of life changes. Consider resisting the temptation to sit in front of the TV and over-eat or smoke cigarettes while congratulating yourself for staying clean!

Now, I understand that the very idea of real physical exercise may sound intimidating to you if you never considered such activity during your days as an addict. It was like that for me at first too. But I'll tell you how naturally the shift happened for me so maybe you can see a similar pathway ahead for you as well.

After my marriage ended I found myself living as a single mom with my daughters Brie and Kara in a new house, in a new neighborhood in Denver. I chose the house in part because it was across the street from the elementary school the girls would be attending, and when I was scouting the neighborhood I noticed a YMCA nearby. Out of curiosity, I walked in one day to check out the programs available. The one that caught my eye was a master's swim workout. Hmmm. I did know how to swim, thanks to my dad teaching me as a young child. The team met at 5 a.m., but I was up by then thanks to the early-morning awakening from my low-grade depression. (No, I never took antidepressant medication. I have no objection to antidepressants for others, as long as we do not collude to make them "the answer". The treatment for depression is so much more involved than just taking a pill! I knew my depression was not the kind that would respond to medication and I knew, on some level, that I had a lot of work to do, a lot of re-solving; I created my own antidepressants: endorphins from exercise.) I did not need to get the kids ready for school and myself prepared for work until closer to 7. I knew nothing about competitive swimming, but back in high school I did play field hockey, lacrosse, and basketball. Maybe I was an athlete waiting to happen.

So I approached the master's swim coach. "What do I need to do first?" I asked. "Well, it would help to get a swim suit," laughed Andy, who referred me to some of the other women swimmers who could fill me in on suits, goggles, caps, etc. And so it began. After briefing my neighbors on my plan, I would lock the house and leave the kids inside while I zipped the few blocks to the Y for a swim before the sun rose. In case they woke up before I returned to get them ready for school and would run into my room to jump on my bed with me, per our usual morning ritual, I would leave a picture of a fish on my pillow so they would remember where I was. The kids also noticed that my habit of sneaking cigarettes in the garage soon ceased. My endorphins were doing their job! Five weeks after starting practice, I competed in a 1650-yard race, the swimmer's mile. I was hooked! For the next 15 years I stuck with that swim team, as well as finding additional physical activities, only leaving because I moved from the Denver area to western Colorado. I'm still friends with many of the men and women on that team.

So where will your endorphins take you? I invite you to start with exercise that fits who you are: walking, riding a bike, going to a gym, swimming, loading an exercise DVD in your home and following along, etc. You don't have to tell yourself you're doing this to lose weight, or to look better to friends, or to pass some test. You are exercising and making endorphins because it supports your Phase I Recovery. Don't you want to do everything possible to help that cause?

Feel free to refer to your Higher Power by any name you choose: force of the Universe; collective good; positive energy.

Lesson #14
ASSIGN A CONCEPT OF GOD YOU CAN BELIEVE IN

Working the Twelve Steps, along with the act of attending meetings and connecting with your recovery sponsor, is so integral to your overall Phase I Recovery that I'm going to devote the next several lessons to strategies, tips, and ideas that will assist you in doing this vital work. We'll start with a further look at the issue of the "G" word in recovery.

Have you been trying to apply the Steps in your life for weeks or even months but you're still struggling with the idea of accepting a concept of a God or Higher Power you can relate to and believe in? For many addicts, embracing a Higher Power is a natural process, but for others it can be a stumbling block, tripping them up at Step 2—came to believe that a Power greater than ourselves could restore us to sanity—or making them wary of even attending recovery meetings. If you find yourself wrestling with this God talk, I'd like to offer some reminders and reassurances that may be helpful.

First, understand that thousands of addicts who have successfully maintained recovery initially resisted this part of the program, and I include myself in their ranks! Share your concerns, and your doubts, with those who have been there. You will receive many more accounts and tips than I could possibly explain here. Next, keep in mind that the Twelve Steps in no way issue a command to adopt any particular religious practice or concept. You are free to call upon the idea, definition, or image of God that strikes a chord for you. I bet that somewhere in the recesses of your being you may be able to find one, if you sincerely look for it. Again, talk to other addicts in the recovery meetings you attend. Read as much recovery literature as you can get your hands on. And, if necessary, start by pretending that there is a God.

69

What if you are carrying some negative concept of God from childhood—a harsh, judgmental, punishing God who would never like you, let alone bother to listen to you or help you? Discard that image! Fire that god!! Start over, and feed, water, and grow any useful seed you may still have. Many people find that they relate to the Judeo-Christian God concept that's more prevalent in the Western hemisphere, but for many other people Eastern religions work well. Others turn to nature and spirituality without religion. Find something that fits for you. Work on a concept of a God with whom you can have a relationship. Assign qualities that resonate with you. Maybe there really is a loving, caring Higher Power that can work to help you stay clean for now—some entity watching over you that wants to keep you alive for some reason. Fake it until you make it in terms of believing in Him, Her, or It. Pray, meditate, say Hare Krishna's, do whatever works for the moment. Your concept will evolve if you allow it to.

Feel free to refer to your Higher Power by any name you choose: force of the Universe; collective good; positive energy. At the end of AA meetings, attendees often stand and recite "The Lord's Prayer." Children attending with their parents often make this innocent substitution in the words: "Our Father who art in heaven, Howard be thy name." Many of us who have heard this reference decided to begin calling God "Howard," which worked as a more comfortable, less ritualized sense of God.

The point is that there is a Higher Power and it is not you. You are simply not the center of the universe. And one way or another, you need to come face to face with the simple reality that as an addict, you can't do this recovery thing alone. You may find yourself saying or thinking, "I can do this myself." But if you could, you would have just stopped using drugs with no problem long ago, right? "I can do it myself" might have been charming when we were two years old, but when we were using drugs it became an empty refrain. When we hit rock bottom, beaten into a state of reasonableness, we finally saw where "I can do it myself" got us.

Two year olds grow up, eventually accepting help from parents, teachers, coaches, and friends. Addicts, too, need to grow up, and that means accepting help where it is most needed. Remember, we addicts

70

are different from casual druggies or social drinkers. If we really want recovery, we need specific solutions. We need structure. Sure, calling only upon other people may work for a while to help you stay clean, but eventually there will come a time when you are not able to use them...you have to get a God. And rest assured that whatever concept of a God you agree on to get started, there's a very good chance that it will evolve as your Phase I Recovery takes hold. Almost everything in your life will be evolving. That's one of the wonderful things about this journey!

Those of us in recovery have found that if we are using anything mind altering, we are, "cut off from the sunlight of the spirit."

Lesson #15
UNDERSTAND THAT THE VOID CAN ONLY BE FILLED BY SOMETHING SPIRITUAL

There's another side to this need for a concept of God or Higher Power during Phase I Recovery. Yes, turning to a Higher Power is essential in gaining the strength and courage to stay clean, to having a chance to claim physical, emotional, and spiritual health and well-being. But as you know by now, recovery may begin with getting clean but it sure doesn't end there. The Phase I Recovery journey is long and full of new pathways to discover and explore. As you continue to travel this new terrain, you will find that so much of the potential in front of you relies on filling that *void* you have experienced for far, far too long.

The *void* is really what addiction is all about. It's the emptiness that we tried to fill up, mostly with substances or obsessive, compulsive processes. The momentary satisfaction from whatever we keep reaching for evaporates like dry ice after a few minutes. The "thing" we thought would do the trick is never enough. So we keep searching, and reaching. Sometimes we simply grab onto stuff: more pairs of shoes; more magazines; more gadgets for all our techno aids. We focus on stuff instead of the people around us. We're still trying to fill up the *void*. And it still doesn't work. The *void*, that hole in our gut, that gnawing feeling of emptiness, the vacancy, the unoccupied space in us that contains nothing, that fills us with pain, wants…something else. Those who have found the way to fill it tell us that it's really our need for a human level of spirituality. Whatever your religious or spiritual beliefs happen to be, I'd invite you to at least consider this question: Could it be that a major reason for your struggles during all that time you used drugs, and for any discontent you have been experiencing early in recovery, is that you have been missing God terribly? Yes, we're back to the "G" word, to a Higher Power, to

73

having some concept of God you can accept and call upon, and even form a relationship with.

Those of us in recovery have found that if we are using anything mind altering, we are, "cut off from the sunlight of the spirit." In other words, if I'm just into me all the time, I can't experience the spiritual side of life around me. I'll keep searching for something else to substitute for it. Wouldn't it be nice to begin to allow some of that sunlight in? Do you have a sense for how you might do it?

I'll tell you how that sunlight of the spirit began to cast its rays on me. After I had been working on my recovery for a while, and slowly allowing myself to at least consider the possibility of the existence of God, I began doing some mountain hiking and climbing. With swimming, I had already begun to find a new outlet for desperately needed physical activity, but mountain climbing took me, you might say, to a whole new level. After all, I lived in mountain country. Colorado has 54 peaks over 14,000 feet and making the decision to climb them all is a tantalizing ambition for many Coloradans. I joined their numbers—and believe me, I paid the price! Lots of physical pain, a ton of doubt, scary moments caught in lightning storms. But I also reaped the rewards—the big ones.

On each of my climbs, I found myself getting closer to God. When I got caught in a storm and didn't think I'd get through, but I did, that was God helping me to safety. When the pain swept through my body like fire, but I somehow endured it and kept climbing, that was God giving me the strength. And maybe most of all, when I simply paused a moment and breathed in a gorgeous view, that especially was God! I mean, how can you stand high on a mountain after all the sweat and anguish it took to get there, breathe in fresh air, look out for miles and miles, and not have a sense that there's got to be a God of some kind out there? I can't explain it, didn't plan it, didn't even consciously ask for it when I began climbing those mountains. It's just that whenever I aimed my sights on a new peak and said, "Let's do it," I felt close to this new sense of God, my climbing buddy. And each time I came back from a day on the mountains, I felt another chunk or two of that formally great big, insurmountable *void* chip away.

Might there be an experience of a God that will do that for you? There is a world full of possibilities. Look around at what you already have in your life that you can take in and appreciate in a new way. Is there anything that, at any point in your life, filled you with a sense of mystery and awe? Seek it again. Is there some new activity you're ready to try that has the potential to stir your soul? Try it now. Listen closely. Your *void* may be calling you to somewhere new, a place where it may at last begin to be filled.

When you try to go it alone early in recovery, choosing not to seek out more mates, you risk giving yourself the same negative, repetitive messages that weighed you down when you were using drugs.

Lesson #16
PEOPLE ARE STRONG MEDICINE

We're not alone. We say it often in recovery meetings because people grappling with the challenges of early recovery really need to hear it...and know how true it really is. Wherever you are in finding your way in Phase I Recovery, hopefully you have discovered that no matter what you may be going through, or what you fear will happen next, there's always someone who can relate to your feelings, to your situation, to your desire to not hurt inside anymore. You need and deserve many people who understand, who have been where you are emotionally, and who will listen.

I was recently watching that 1980s box office hit movie *Crocodile Dundee* and was struck by a scene with Sue, the reporter, and Mick, hero of the Australian outback. Mick had come to New York City and was trying to make sense of American ways. Sue was explaining to him why a friend was seeing a psychiatrist.

Mick: "Doesn't she have any mates?"

Sue: "I guess there aren't any shrinks in Walkabout."

Mick: "If you have a problem in Walkabout, you tell Wally, he tells everyone in town, brings it out in the open and there's no more problem."

Sue: "We could all use more mates."

That's especially true in recovery. When you feel engulfed with problems over how to navigate your new life free of addiction, telling others about those problems eases the burden. And when you reach out in your recovery community, you find an ample supply of "mates" who can be objective, non-judgmental, and not willing to cosign your bull----. They will be able to listen to you and help you see your part in each of your problems. Of course, you will find that the usefulness of the sharing is directly proportional to the completeness and honesty of the information you provide. If you tell your listener what happened to you but don't get to how you contributed to the situation, you won't receive much useful feedback. It works the same way in any life situation. If you tell someone your car is a problem—too noisy, broken or malfunctioning parts, whatever—and ask them what to do, they may give you certain advice. If, however, you are honest with them and admit that you have not done the proper maintenance, they may give you completely different feedback, helping you to see how the car is not the problem…you are. See how that can work in all your issues?

When you try to go it alone early in recovery, choosing not to seek out more mates, you risk giving yourself the same negative, repetitive messages that weighed you down when you were using drugs. Your brain gets stuck in old thinking, and your behavior is based on outmoded ways of looking at yourself and others. Those in recovery can help you see everything, including yourself, in a new perspective. This is especially true for sponsors.

Your sponsor is your one-on-one checkpoint, the person primarily entrusted with supporting you in attending to the most essential parts of your Phase I Recovery. A good sponsor will help you get focused and stay focused on the Twelve Steps, helping to guide you through them one by one and assisting you with specific assignments. Your sponsor will encourage you to attend meetings regularly. He or she can be one of your main confidantes, someone you can trust with your secrets that finally need to be aired for you to gain physical, emotional, and spiritual health. Your sponsor can truly be your lifeline, as Shelley was to me.

One of my first sponsors during my tumultuous early recovery phase, Shelley stood by me while I tried to make sense of Step 4: "Made a searching and fearless moral inventory of ourselves." In other words, I had to remember, relive, write down, and then look at my part in many years of resentments and bitterness. Ultimately, this was a liberating process, and I am eternally grateful for having struggled thought it. Since that first time, I have repeated this step as needed.

Shelley got to listen to me procrastinate. An administrative assistant at a Denver hospital, she finally invited me to do the writing in her office so I would just get it done. So there I'd be, sprawled out on her office floor, scratching away with pen and pad, my face contorting with agony. And Shelley just let me be who I needed to be. When someone would enter the office she'd calmly advise the visitor, "Oh, don't mind her. She's part of the furniture. Just step over her." Thanks in large part to the help from Shelley and others who had been there, I made it through my first round of doing the fourth step.

Today, I value the sponsor relationship more than ever. Whenever I see a new patient seeking guidance for addiction and recovery, I immediately ask, "Do you have a sponsor? If you have one, have you been meeting with them regularly?" If the answers come back "no," I bust them. "Get a sponsor now," I say, or "Call that sponsor you've lost touch with today." Over the years, I have sponsored many women. Joanie jokes that I have been her "temporary" sponsor for the fifteen years she has been in recovery. Others have asked me to sponsor them but never called; still others call and accept the assignments I give to do the steps, but never do them. A sponsor can only help and "carry the message"; he or she cannot "carry the addict."

A healthcare professional who actually understands addiction and recovery can serve as another valuable mate. Therapists are trained to help you look at yourself, within the context of a supportive and encouraging relationship. Some recovering addicts with established religious roots may reach out to religious counselors. Others find they draw the greatest strength and hope not from meeting with individuals alone but from soaking up the environment where groups of people are sharing their stories of drinking and drugging, and the road to recovery they are seeking to follow. I have seen this often. Here's an inspiring example:

A retired physician had been referred to me with a problem, which I quickly determined was sex addiction. His wife had caught him using porn and visiting prostitutes. When he first entered my office, I made sure to look him in the eyes and say, "Nice to meet you." I wanted him to know that I was not there to judge him but rather to help and support him. Having a woman treat him with respect surprised him because he had lost respect for himself. As he sobbed, I said calmly, "You can recover." I connected him with a small group made up mostly of my patients who were regularly meeting as a Sex

Addicts recovery group. Before this retired physician felt ready to show up, two of the men met with him for coffee and reassured him that he was not the only one to have gone through this experience. They gave him the confidence and comfort to attend the meetings, which happened to convene in my professional office on an evening when I was not there. I told the owner of the offices in our building that these guys were holding my "Board of Directors meeting." Actually, they were mates, helping to support one another's recovery.

Recently I was seeing Annemarie, a 27-year-old patient with an eating disorder. Unfortunately, the nearest eating disorder recovery meetings were several hours' drive from her home. "It's not going to be enough just to see me once in a week in my office," I told her. "You need to attend other recovery meetings, like AA, that are within reach for you." When she refused, I made a decision: I took her to a meeting with me. After that, she would at least go alone to women-only recovery meetings. And when I traveled, I agreed to serve as one of Annemarie's lifelines. So while I was spending a few weeks in Arizona visiting my daughter, I was not surprised when Annemarie called. I knew that it was a night she had agreed to attend a regular meeting.

"Did you go?" I asked. Though she said yes, I could tell that something was amiss. "Annemarie, do you have any of your trigger foods with you now?" I asked. Yes, she had bought large amounts of her favorite goodies to binge on after the meeting. "Great," I said, "Do you want me to hold on while you throw them out?" It was snowing that evening, and it took Annemarie several trips to the dumpster to deposit all her binge food. She didn't like me doing that to her, but I was proud of her. It was not anything I learned in medical school that allowed me to sense, even over the phone, that she was in trouble; it was my own recovery. A physician or therapist who has been there has an extra capacity to help his or her patients.

Whatever you choose in your efforts to reach out to others for help, apply the principles we discussed previously, HOW: Honesty, Open-mindedness, and Willingness. No matter how different these new mates or helpers may first appear to you, remember this: these are the people who truly can provide you with the best medicine for recovery.

Lesson #17
TAKING MORAL INVENTORY DOES NOT MEAN BLAMING YOURSELF

I'd like to follow up on that image from the previous lesson of me agonizing to work on that "fearless and thorough moral inventory" of myself in accordance with Step 4 of the Twelve Steps. I need to be very clear about the purpose of this process. Taking moral inventory does not mean grading or blaming yourself and all your life experiences. Do you know that? And if you have doubted it even when you were reminded of this by your sponsor or another supporter in your recovery program, stop doubting. You are not setting out to put yourself down. You are engaged in an endeavor that can set you free.

Taking moral inventory is a way we can look at ourselves and get free from our past. Many addicts clog their lives with resentment, anger, old pain...and new pain. We are in bondage to our thoughts, slaves to our feelings. We allow outside stuff to occupy space in our brain, rent-free, to keep us unhappy and potentially make us drink or use again. When we are thinking about old events, re-feeling (the word resentment is derived from the Latin verb sentir, to feel) old anger, we are tied to that event and time, and we miss the joy of being free in today.

Make no mistake: the path to this freedom via Step 4 is vital work. In fact, the well-worn saying in recovery groups speaks to its pivotal role in recovery: "One, two, three, drink," goes the commentary on what happens to people early in recovery who are not willing to plow through Step 4. Experience does indeed suggest that if you only do Steps 1, 2, and 3, without continuing through the rest of the program, you quite likely will relapse.

So you need to do it, but it doesn't need to do you in. The reality is that you are being directed by Step 4 to look at yourself, which

81

I know tends to bring out the "But it's not me!" refrain, followed by the list: it's my sick, abusive family; it's my partner; it's my boss; it's my co-worker; it's this crazy country, etc. Well, those other people are not here, and you are. You are the one stuck in ongoing discomfort from your anger and resentments. You can't change them, but you can change yourself and your reaction to them, all of them.

If you haven't taken on the real work of Step 4 yet, getting started may be easier than you think. Many workbooks and resource guides, including directions found in the AA Big Book, will help walk you through it. Your sponsor can help. Remember first to KISS: Keep It Simple, Sweetie! If your moral inventory gets too complicated and convoluted, it may become too difficult for you to finish. The point is to move on and do the work, not to obsess about the past.

First, make a list of people, places, institutions, or whatever, against whom you feel anger and resentment. Include places, like the college you dropped out of, or institutions like religion or the IRS. Family members will likely have a place near the top, and that's okay. Get it all down on paper...just a list. Then write a few sentences about why you have negative feelings and thoughts related to this person, place, etc. Write as much or as little as you want. Just do it. If you need to expand, now or later, do that, too. If you tap into more anger at the same person the day after you make an entry, write about him or her again.

After sifting through and recording your resentments, write down how these things you have referenced have affected you. Maybe it's your relationships, your sense of self, your job status, maybe even your finances, etc. You do not have to do this perfectly. It is not for publication or a PhD thesis.

Now comes the personal side, where you look for your part in these resentments. After all, you did participate in them most of the time. If you are honest and careful, or have someone helping you to be honest and careful, you can begin to see your contributions. Caution: if you were abused as a child, you did not do anything to cause that! And even if you were randomly assaulted as an adult, that is not your fault either. We can, however, learn from everything that has happened to us. Sometimes we learn that our part is simply in choosing unhealthy people to keep in our lives. Other times, though, we know we did harm to someone. This is simply admitting the truth, without the need to justify or counter-attack. That's your past. You have a present and a future, and those old stand-by tactics don't belong. Believe me, that's liberating!

So while you're letting go of that tempting reflex to blame others, also make sure to refuse to blame yourself. You have a disease and you are doing the courageous work to get well. Rather than blame or judgment, you deserve lots of encouragement—both from your helpers and from yourself.

You will find that some amends are obvious. If you stole something before you entered recovery, return it now.

Lesson #18
MAKING AMENDS CAN REALLY GET YOU HIGH

As an addict dedicated to your recovery, I trust that you are working all the Twelve Steps in order. Doing that is essential! In our exploration of key issues and reminders in Phase I Recovery, we will continue to highlight some specific steps where many on this journey tend to hit a major stumbling block. Please note that I am not providing a comprehensive walk through all the steps. In spite of the fact that they are ALL important, I am only briefly discussing a few of the steps. For many in recovery, a barrier emerges when they go about making amends. I'll offer some assistance that may make the ride smoother.

Let's look more closely, then, at Step 8 (Made a list of all persons we had harmed, and became willing to make amends to them all) and Step 9 (Made direct amends to such people whenever possible, except when to do so would injure them or others). A common defensive response often sounds something like this: "Harmed? Who have I harmed? Not me! I have never done anything to anyone; well, at least I never physically hurt anybody. I would never hit, push, bite or fight. And I never did anything mean; well, except when they were mean to me first. I didn't shout or name-call; well, not usually, except maybe that time...but I was angry so it doesn't count and besides, he deserved it. Well, yes, I had a glass or two of wine when he made me so mad... but that had nothing to do with it."

Sound like any of that might apply, at least a little, to anything you have said or thought? As addicts, usually we are unaware of the harm we do while we are doing it. It's not until later, perhaps at a more selfless time when we are clearing our minds in Phase I Recovery, that we really understand how deeply what we do affects others. We human beings are very good at justification, retaliation, and denial. So think for a moment. Is there any chance you have ever done anything unkind, maybe even harmful to family? To parents, siblings, spouse, children? How about extended family? Friends? Coworkers, neighbors, strangers? Anyone else? Ever behave rudely or selfishly in traffic, in line at the grocery store, or anywhere else you are somewhat anonymous?

Is there any chance that you have been one of those countless addicts who are good at putting on a façade for the public? You dressed perfectly, every hair in place, when you were away from home, wearing the "I am perfect and so is all in my life" mask, saving your biting comments and controlling, passive-aggressive, even vicious behavior for your family. Of course, you also need to consider the more outright harms: theft, cheating, dishonesty, etc. Even little omissions can be damaging: not acknowledging someone's existence either in person or by not returning a call, snubs and rejections of any kind. All of this behavior harms the person committing the act—you—as well as the recipient of your actions.

When you sincerely apply yourself to Step 8, you may find yourself with quite a list of persons you have harmed. Believe me, you are not alone in that either! Most addicts have left a long trail of necessary stops to make amends. Now comes the "making direct amends" part of Step 9. You will definitely want to call upon your mates and helpers for this: your sponsor, close friends in recovery, a trusted therapist. But it really does not have to be something that you fear or dread. Consider that the word "amend" means, "make changes, corrections, or improvements." That doesn't sound so painful, does it?

You will find that some amends are obvious. If you stole something before you entered recovery, return it now. A doctor friend of mine stole a piece of equipment from another doctor. He couldn't recall whether he was drunk or stoned at the time of the theft, but even when not acutely intoxicated, he, like all addicts, exercised poor judgment. Also, like all addicts, his world was entirely about him, no thought for anyone else, until he stopped using drugs and began working the steps. Sure, it took courage to finally return that item, but when he did he felt a large weight lift off his shoulders. You can obtain the relief even when the party on the other end no longer exists. I had a friend in recovery who had used bogus forms to steal money from an insurance company for years. When she discovered that the company no longer existed, she made a donation to an appropriate charity. There are numerous stories of amends letters being read at graveside to those who passed on long ago.

More likely, your primary amends will be to people you have harmed. People you know well. People who have loved you. Often simply acknowledging awareness of your part in a destructive relationship to the other person can open the door to repairing that relationship. Other times, though, just coming clean and saying "I'm sorry" is simply not going to get it done. That other person whom you have harmed may have been waiting for years for you to take some responsibility. You can help by listening without judgment to their venting of pent-up frustration, and you can further help by asking, "What can I do to make it right?" Some people you have harmed may simply not accept your attempt at making amends. The other person may just need to sit in her own resentment a while longer, perhaps because of fear, or just being stuck emotionally and spiritually. Do not be discouraged. All you can do is to do the best you can. You cannot fix anyone else, but you can do your part in all relationships.

And you know what? The more you practice making amends, the more natural it becomes. You become freer and lighter as you go along. You begin to see that nobody will have anything to hold over you; your life will be cleaned up and you will have no fear of anyone finding out something. We are just as sick as our secrets, and you won't have secrets. When you quit keeping all that yucky stuff inside, you will have more energy, and you will be more available to help others. You will be experiencing an authentic, natural high. And your spiral upward will be continuing!

Be resourceful, creative and playful. So what if someone laughs at your new tradition? At least they're laughing for the right reasons.

SECTION 3: WELCOMING CHANGE

Lesson #19
START NEW TRADITIONS

I have a confession to make regarding my recovery. All these changes that I am urging you to make to support your Phase I Recovery, including the ones that sound so hard they just make you want to scream or gag, did not come easily for me either. As I began to change, little by little, I was kicking and screaming all the way. After ending my marriage, I was a 34-year-old physician and single mother of two young girls. Wasn't that change enough? What else did I need to do? Answer: Keep doing what I was told regarding the work of recovery by those who had been there and had happy, productive, drug-free lives. I had consciously committed to recovery, yet much of my commitment was a gut level understanding that it was the only choice if I was to live. I was able to feel, to recognize in my innermost soul, that the choices were to change or to die.

Meanwhile, my old drinking and drugging buddies kept waiting for me to get back in the game. Some may still be still waiting! Others who had wished I might someday take this turn toward health and well-being would greet me with the words, "We never thought you would stop...so what do you want to drink?" And then the warm laughs when I would answer, "Tea, please."

Since I knew I couldn't do things the old drinking and drugging ways when it came to socializing and sharing special times such as holidays, I believed others when they told me that I needed to come up with new ways that were emotionally safe. That's how I began to recognize that I had been blessed with the wonderful gift of having a "family of choice." In other words, instead of being trapped in a household with two alcoholic parents and all the yucky stuff that went with that, or unconsciously repeating so much of what I had learned prior to recovery, in childhood, early adulthood and marriage, I was experiencing a new-found freedom of choosing who I wanted to be with and what I wanted to do.

It was an enormous relief not to be keeping the company of others in active addiction. Not only did I not want to be around drinking and drugging, I also immediately noticed other differences. Often active addicts simply do not have the tools to deal constructively with conflict, the capacity to be honest and accepting, or the focus on caring. In contrast, my new friends from the recovery community were easy to be with. These were men and women of all ages and backgrounds who were working hard at their recovery, some doing their own kicking and screaming, but also finding plenty of ways to laugh, to celebrate, to grow, to express gratitude without the use of alcohol and other drugs. I could be myself, not have to censor anything, talk about feelings, and relax more than ever without the use of mind-altering chemicals. These were the people I wanted to be around all the time. This was my family of choice.

One of the many wonderful traditions in the recovery program is reaching out to one another to share birthdays and holidays, as well as the major celebrations that come with reaching an anniversary date of being clean. These were the new traditions that I was starting in my first year or two of recovery, and they provided both a stabilizing force and feelings of joy.

Let me illustrate this point by taking you back to Christmas Eve 1985. Janice, one of my new friends who was a few years ahead of me in her recovery, hosted a potluck party. Over the course of the holiday evening, more than 100 fellow recovering addicts came and went. I took my daughters with me because as a new family of three we were especially hungry for new traditions for the holidays. Many of my friends already knew Brie and Kara because I had been taking them with me to meetings for well over a year. My girls loved seeing that my friend José, who shared the same anniversary date as mine, had brought dozens of tamales. For a moment I flashed to how Christmas Eve used to look before I entered Phase I Recovery. My ex-husband and I would stay up late putting together the kids' toys, pulling out the stash of cocaine we had set aside to get us through this bout of parental duty....

Yes, it was a fun and lively night at Janice's, the kind of enjoyment that recovering addicts are very good at tapping without drugs. Then, on Christmas morning, I initiated another new tradition with the girls at home. I would hide the last present for each of them, so they had to hunt for them. And I told them that every Christmas they would now get to choose what our family would eat for Christmas dinner. On that Christmas when they chose lasagna and mashed potatoes, I never hesitated. We had come a long way, beginning a journey of new traditions and aware of the new possibilities ahead.

That same opportunity awaits you. What new traditions will help you further mark your new trail along Phase I Recovery? How do you want to observe the holidays? Who do you want to spend birthdays with? If you had routines for specific days and times you would indulge in drinking and drugging in the old days, what new ritual could you begin in that same time slot now?

Be resourceful, creative and playful. So what if someone laughs at your new tradition? At least they're laughing for the right reasons.

So trust me, as you go about your recovery work, it's good to be seen. People are not waiting to judge or ridicule you.

Lesson #20
REALIZE THAT IT'S OKAY
TO BE SEEN

"But someone will see me there!" goes the popular excuse for not attending recovery meetings. I often hear this as an excuse from my patients, and I have my ready responses:

• Meetings are often held in churches or other public venues. Most meetings are at night, so it's unlikely that anyone except the attendees will see you there. During daytime hours, if there are other people in that building for other purposes, they aren't likely to know why you're there.

• When you walk into a meeting room, everyone is there for the same reason. So if someone there recognizes you, that person most likely is also an addict in recovery—and you're seeing them too! My husband Erik used to be a bouncer at a bar before he landed in recovery. At one of his first meetings, he encountered someone he used to regularly bounce out of the bar! They were both seen, and it was totally okay. They were coming together in a new way, for a common purpose.

• You're just not that important. People don't care about what you're up to. Your neighbors and co-workers are too busy with their own lives, too embroiled with their own drama to pay much attention to yours.

And yet, I understand where the excuse-makers are coming from because I've been there myself. Oh, I had no problem sitting with the street people and the bikers in all those inner-city Denver meetings that I gravitated to in my first weeks of recovery. Many became long-lasting friends. I was comfortable around them because they were real. As with most recovering men and women, regardless of education, socio-economic status, race, or anything else, there was minimal pretense. The "what you see is what you get" attitude was reassuring and comforting. If others were being themselves, I could too. Acceptance of others makes self-acceptance easier and vice-versa.

Even in Denver, though, I didn't dare mention to my new friends that I was a doctor. I really wasn't ready to be seen and known for who I was. I remember how Rick and Kim admitted to me much later, after I had "come out" as a doctor in recovery, that they had been absolutely convinced that I was a hooker. Who else would be so secretive about not discussing work or giving them my phone number, even though I readily accepted theirs? Hmmm. What was I afraid of? Being known for the real me? I had no idea at the time who that was. Maybe I was just having the residual of cocaine paranoia.

I had heard from someone who ought to know that no one would care or pay attention to my profession, that it would not be an issue at all. Doctor Joe, that physician I had met through Blair, my catalyst for beginning this journey, delivered that reassurance. Weeks before I finally went to my first N.A. meeting, Doctor Joe listened to my fears about potentially being known as a doctor addict.

"Dawn, don't worry," he said. "When they find out you're a doctor, it's not any different from being at a cocktail party where people know what you do and ask you medical questions."

Ah, but I did worry about people knowing I was a doctor in recovery. And I worried more about people in my neighborhood, maybe even my own patients, learning about my addiction. At first I didn't even realize there were recovery meetings in my community of Evergreen, but when I did find out about those local meetings it took me some time to get up the nerve to show up at one.

The meeting site was at a church up in the hills, and only a handful of attendees were present. In other words, I had nowhere to hide. And right away I recognized her: Joyce, a woman from town—and one of my current patients. I took a deep breath, walked over, and sat down right beside her.

"Hi," said Joyce. "I didn't know you were a part of this too."

"Well, I'm new, about 90 days, " I said, making eye contact, forcing myself to be direct and clear and pretending I was not sacred...of what? Of being real? Ugh. One of the enormous gifts of recovery is being real, terrifying as it sometimes is!

"Oh, I've been sober for five years," she said. "It's right on my patient chart."

And it hit me—I had never even noticed it. I was not even aware that one of my regular patients was an alcoholic in recovery. I regarded her as simply a very pleasant woman I treated for upper respiratory ailments. Medical students are not taught to look at the information about alcohol on charts and on those questionnaires patients fill out. We are more likely to ask about smoking history, because telling people to stop smoking is acceptable and few doctors smoke now. But doctors do drink. In fact, some say that the doctor's definition of drinking too much is simply drinking more than he or she drinks. Talk about denial!

So my patient and I didn't say much more, but as the meeting progressed I surprised myself that I was not horrified at being "seen" at all. In fact, it was a relief. I said to myself, "Okay, if anyone who meets me knows who I am, and knows that I'm a doctor in recovery, that's just the way it is. I'm okay the way I am." I was even more surprised, and pleased, to find that when I saw Joyce as a patient again, we were both more comfortable with our doctor-patient relationship. She was just one more mate.

That chance encounter with Joyce marked a turning point: from then on I would confidently attend meetings near my home, near my work, near my family's homes, wherever I was. I told anyone who asked what I did for work, relating to being a doc as simply a job. Interestingly, as I had been told, no one cared! At my regular meetings they gave me a new name, to distinguish me from two other women named Dawn who attended the same meetings. So I was "DocDawn," rather than "Milk Truck Dawn" or "Dawn, Mother of Twins." This was 25 years ago and I remain friends with both of these Dawns. All three of us have beaten the odds: none has relapsed. I suspect this is in part due to us forming solid relationships with one another and with others in recovery. I rarely just went to a meeting; usually a group of us from the meeting would follow up by going out to eat or at least for coffee. Most summer weekends included a party, dance, campout, or other activity, all ways to learn to play without alcohol or other drugs. And we did it all without any concerns for letting others in our circle know who we were, what our past was, or what we did for a living.

That name DocDawn, and my identity as a woman and doctor in recovery, has stuck with me. So trust me, as you go about your recovery work, it's good to be seen. People are not waiting to judge or ridicule you. More likely they will respond with encouragement, support, and often admiration. That's nothing to be afraid of, is it?

Lesson #21
DON'T KEEP YOUR RECOVERY A SECRET FROM YOUR KIDS

If you are walking the path of Phase I Recovery and you have children, you may be tempted to keep your experience of rebuilding your life mostly out of sight and out of mind from them. Depending on their age, you may fear that they would not understand, or that their questions would make you squirm. From what I know and have witnessed, however, keeping your recovery a secret would be a mistake.

Think about this. Your children sure knew something was wrong when you were drinking and using drugs, even if it wasn't spoken of then, so they need to know that you have taken on the challenge of doing something right now. You can reveal it as simply as, "Mom was sick and now she's doing what she needs to do to get well" and then patiently explain about meetings and the other components of your recovery program in an age-appropriate manner. Again, your sponsor and other friends from your recovery community will be happy to help you find the right approach.

Your kids need to know because while you have gotten rid of the drugs, it's not likely that you have swiftly plowed through all the emotional upheaval that comes with waking up to your addiction. So they're going to see you irritable, depressed, or afraid, and you're not going to be able to be fully present to them every day during the stormy weather of Phase I Recovery. Explain to them why this is so, and assure them that you are taking the steps (literally!) to get healthier and healthier.

For my daughters Brie and Kara, life soon after I had quit drinking and drugging was about watching me try to navigate both my recovery and then, in less than a year, my separation and divorce from their father. Our house was often filled with tears (mostly mine) and stress (mostly for Brie, a second grader). Truthfully, I was still not doing a very good job as a mother in the beginning. "Parenting is just too hard," I would lament, as I observed Brie taking on a maternal role with her little sister, only three years younger. Brie, seven at the time I separated from their father, actually gave Kara her bath some nights. When I was using, I could cover my anxiety and confusion with a few drinks, some marijuana, or a line of cocaine. Now I had to pretend to know how to be an adult and a mother, never having had a good role model for either. Parenting presents difficulties for the healthiest of people; for me, it was as if I had to learn everything anew and deal with reality, normal people and ordinary tasks sober. Scary!

For those of you who may be very secure and cannot relate to the idea of being scared of ordinary people, especially your children's teachers and other parents, this must sound pretty strange. Just imagine a 14 year old trying to act like an adult while doing something like divorcing, moving, buying a house in a new community, and signing two children up for school. At the time, I was 14 emotionally and fearful of anything new. When I put on my doctor mask and went to work, I felt very secure. I knew how to be a doctor, had been trained to do that, and I did it well (though I was not as intuitive and emotionally in touch as I am now). I did not know how to be an ordinary human being; that was the scary part. Having grown up with a mother who was either drunk or irritable and angry, I did not know how to parent. New and scary!

One thing I was clear about: my commitment to attend recovery meetings several times a week was not going to change when the girls were staying with me. They spent one night a week and every other weekend with their dad, so those times became my main times to do anything I needed to do without them. During the rest of the week we had a choice, and I involved them in the decision: they could stay home with a sitter or go to the meetings with me. They voted for coming along to these gatherings of "alcies" and "druggies", never once choosing a baby sitter. Looking back now over 28 years later, I'd say that was one of the best choices we made as a family. Most of the meetings I attended had no policy on children and no one complained as long as children did not distract. My little girls a distraction? No way. They would just crawl up into one of the familiar laps, treated as part of the family from the beginning, or they would sit quietly working on their coloring books as they whispered to one another about whether this might be an anniversary for one of the attendees because that meant cake! And of course they loved the Sunday morning meetings held in a corner of a local restaurant: pancakes!

Kara was only a couple of years out of diapers then, but a few years ago she walked back into the same restaurant as an adult, wanting pancakes for breakfast. She remembered that is where I would be at 7:30 Sunday morning. The kids also enjoyed the potluck parties and holiday open houses hosted by recovering addicts, not just for the food but for the company. They were finding friendship and camaraderie in the recovery community too. Sometimes "our" new friends would swoop into our home in early evening and announce, "We're going out—the pizza's on me."

Of course, life in DocDawn's house during Phase I Recovery was not all about meetings and Mom's emotional tight-rope. We had lots of fun, because I had more room for that too. The girls and I welcomed into our home four cats, assorted pet mice adopted from Brie's second grade class, and a series of rabbits. We also had Tinkerbelle, our three-toed Florida box turtle who lived with us for 24 years until her death from natural causes. I finally had the energy and location for a vegetable garden and my addict friend Rex, an above-the-knee amputee, helped me with the digging and planting. Rex has since died from relapse to this disease, leaving many who loved him during his twenty years of participation in recovery.

The girls knew I was not drinking and delighted in helping me read labels in the grocery store. Anything that listed alcohol as an ingredient was not welcome in our home, and they proudly participated in that new rule. Even as the years went by they would still respect it, going as far as to ask their adult friends to not bring alcohol into our home. One guest offered to bring wine to Kara's bridal shower in our home and the girls asked her not to do that out of respect for me! More was happening than just a healthier life for me; the girls were becoming sensitive, aware, and caring young ladies. None of that would have happened had I tried to act out the "drama" of my recovery mostly off stage from my children.

So if you have kids, don't leave them guessing what's going on between scenes. Show them who you are and share the courageous choices you are making every day for yourself, and for them.

Lesson #22
ACCEPT THIS BONUS POINT: YOU'RE BETTER AT YOUR JOB

So you're choosing healthier ways for yourself and for your family as you follow your recovery program. You are becoming more real around the people close to you. Want to know about another benefit of sticking with the path of Phase I Recovery? If you have not already discovered it, you also are likely to find you are more effective in whatever work you do. There are many reasons for that.

For starters, you're no longer coming to work high, hung over, or sleep deprived from binging. You're also not wasting time plotting lies or covering your tracks because of whatever mayhem you've been causing in your professional, social, or home life. In other words, when you come to your job now, you really show up. You are also more present, more alert, and more intuitive. You see and react to things you never would have noticed in the midst of your addiction. Experts say we only have access to ten per cent of our brains, and when you were obscuring much of that with mind-altering drugs, that didn't leave much for real productivity and creativity, did it? Now you can take on your work assignments and direction with that full ten per cent operative and functioning.

And you know what else? You're just smarter from doing the emotional and spiritual work of recovery and hanging out with people who have learned deeper life lessons than others could even imagine. Early in my recovery I used to tell those who knew me that I had learned more about myself, and life, in the first eight days of recovery than I had in eight years of therapy. Nothing that's happened in the 28 years since then would lead me to discount that claim. And not only do you take more creativity and life learning back to your work, you also carry with you the active, ongoing support of all your new friends in

101

recovery. Your mates are cheering you in every aspect and dimension of your life, and that certainly includes what you do to earn a living and make a difference in our world. They can help you see your true gifts, fueling your own instincts and drive to enhance the work you do or consider new work and career directions.

I remember that moment after one of my first meetings when I was told by Dee, a therapist several years sober, that as a physician I would someday be in a position to help many people with addiction recovery. She was one of the first to encourage me. My first sponsor, Linda, who held a doctorate in education, once pulled me aside and said, "Dawn, you can be helpful to any new person walking through that door—more than me. Since I've been in recovery five years, new people can't relate to me as well as they can relate to you with your five weeks of recovery."

It didn't take long to see the evidence. After I had moved to the Denver area I gave a talk at Lutheran Hospital, where I was on staff, and told my story of addiction and recovery to help educate other doctors about the disease of addiction. Soon after that talk, many of the physicians on staff began referring to me their alcoholic and drug addicted patients, as well as their friends and family. Also, many new patients sought me out because they had heard something of what I had gone through: growing up in an alcoholic family; surviving two suicide attempts and hatching a plan for a third; 20 years of active addiction; a divorce early in my recovery. Doctors and patients all trusted that I could understand whatever hurricane hit them. For myself, I found that I could offer not only sound medical advice related to addiction and recovery, but also the encouragement and hope that we share with one another in recovery meetings. I was simply a lot more empathic and connected than ever before. I understood those who had been or still were living on the edge of life and death. How could I not?

I recall one early experience with Margie, a woman who had recently begun a recovery program. She sought me out because "I heard about a doctor in the area who was in recovery." As she confided me in, Margie had a dreadful fear of doctors. A victim of childhood sexual abuse, she had been on and off with alcohol and prescription drugs. She just didn't trust what doctors would say or do.

Once we had established a rapport as human beings, beyond a basic doctor-patient relationship, she allowed me to treat an assortment of minor medical problems she had long ignored.

Just by being myself, I was suddenly helping people in new ways. You don't have to be a doctor to become more effective in whatever work you do to have positive influence on those around you and to help others simply by being yourself. Embrace those opportunities!

This is the picture that I'm committed to changing in the work that I do every day as an MD Addictionist.

PART II

BEWARE: YOUR DOCTOR MAY BE YOUR PUSHER

And the more docs know about addiction and recovery, the better able they will be to guide addicts in those healthy choices.

Lesson #23
DOCTORS, LEARN THE TWELVE STEPS!

Okay, all you doctors and other healthcare professionals out there, and those of you in recovery who see them, I told you back in the Introduction that I would have a whole lot to say about what doctors do not know about addiction and recovery. I warned you that I'd be critical at times. Well, that time has come. In this next series of lessons I will be shedding light on the myths, the misunderstandings, and the mistakes that derail healthcare providers' often well-intentioned efforts at assisting women and men wrestling with addiction and facing the challenges of both Phase I and Phase II Recovery. I'm going to tell the truth of what I see and hear out there, primarily from my patients and others in the recovering community, about what happens in the offices of doctors of all kinds. Not only sad and unnecessary, ignorance among physicians about the disease of addiction is often life threatening.

This is the picture that I'm committed to changing in the work that I do every day as an MD Addictionist. I'm devoting an entire part of this book toward this effort now because I know that for any addict who seeks to survive Phase I Recovery and thrive in Phase II Recovery, the missteps of their healthcare professionals can stand as a real threat to complicate and interfere with their best efforts. Equipped with accurate information, you can avoid being a victim of a well-meaning but misinformed doctor or therapist. Learn about what you're potentially dealing with in relating to healthcare providers so that you can make the most informed choices. And the more doctors know about addiction and recovery, the better able they will be to guide addicts in those healthy choices.

Before I begin the detailed play by play, I'd like to present a friendly invitation to each and every healthcare professional who may be reading this book—even if it was dropped off to you anonymously by a visitor to your office! Become familiar with the basic philosophies and approach of Twelve Step recovery programs. Begin by learning or re-familiarizing yourself with the Twelve Steps. Remember it's free...and you don't need a prescription. Read the AA Big Book and the NA Basic text. Go to my website (www.docdawn.com) and read the articles. Call or email me for more!

SECTION 4: MISSED SIGNALS

Lesson #24

THE PROBLEM IS THE ADDICT, NOT THE BEHAVIOR

Let's begin our examination into what happens when addicts meet doctors with this burning issue: doctors and other healthcare professionals do not score highly on effectively diagnosing addiction. I'll begin with a common strategy employed by addicts in denial. They're especially good at using it with their spouse or other loved one, but as a doctor you may get wind of it too. The argument goes something like this: "Everyone is addicted to something, right?" As they list all the addictions they have in mind, such as work, or the cell phone, or shopping, their hope is to take the spotlight off their real addiction: alcohol and other substances.

Let's carefully knife our way through the clouds on this argument. Read: "Let's cut through the crap." First, understand this: some people, about 10 or 15 per cent of the population, are addicts. They are susceptible to becoming addicted to any substance they use or process they engage in. The other 85 or 90 per cent of people out there are not addicts. They can safely drink on occasion, or sit for several hours watching TV or playing video games, or even go to the racetrack once in a while, and not risk destructive behavior with adverse consequences or suffer withdrawal when they pull the plug on their favorite activity.

The point is that the addict is the problem, not the process, or even the substance, by itself. A non-addict can have an intense interest in something, perhaps animals, reading, or art. In our Rocky Mountain town of Steamboat Springs, Colorado, the passion du jour is skiing in the winter, cycling in the summer. These endeavors do not typically become destructive. The non-addict does not switch from intense and passionate reading, painting, or skiing to abuse of alcohol or pills. But for an addict, the approach to practically any substance or activity is the same: do it more and more, no matter the harm it may cause, while losing all control along the way. The use of the drug or the process takes on a life of its own, no longer being a choice but rather becoming a compulsion.

Addicts are just different from other people in the kinds of relationships they form with what they put into their bodies and the activities they do. If you ever have the opportunity to listen to an addict, even one in recovery, while trying to explain to a non-addict (spouse, therapist, loved one) how he thinks or used to think about alcohol, drugs, food, or gambling, watch the puzzled look on the non-addict's face. Then watch two addicts talking to each other about the same subject. Notice them nodding their heads, usually laughing at their own bizarre behavior and even finishing each other's sentences? They share the lens of an addict, and that lens colors their perspective, and their choices, about all kinds of things that anyone may label addictive.

Now let's turn to the basic argument that processes and activities as well as substances can become addictive. If you open your dictionary and look at the definition of "addict" as a verb, you will find something like this: "To devote or surrender oneself to something habitually or obsessively." Doesn't that definition fit something like over-eating or playing video games? The answer is that it can—if the person indulging in the behavior also fits the profile of other signs of addictive behavior: lying about the activity or becoming more secretive about it; using it to avoid difficult feelings; neglecting other life responsibilities while engaging more and more in the process; continuing obsessive use of the activity despite relationship problems and other adverse consequences. Adverse consequences of overeating are easy to see, as the evidence is in the body size and other parameters of physical health; adverse consequences of gambling may be financial destruction. But some addictions can go on for many years or even decades, without consequences obvious to others...meanwhile the destruction of relationships and of sense of self are doing their damage.

If you go to my website (www.docdawn.com), you will find that I have provided an extensive list of Process Addictions as well as Substance Addictions. Again, it's critical to keep in mind the distinctions between the two categories. First, those who cease compulsive practices typically do not go through the same physiological symptoms of withdrawal that addicts suffer when they cease drinking or drugging, although they do experience loss. Second, most of these activities that could become Process Addictions, or behavioral addictions, are not inherently harmful in themselves. It is certainly possible to overeat at a party or special event once in a while without tumbling into the kind of overeating habit that can open the gate to the harmful consequences of addiction. But once that gate is opened to an addict, look out! Having worked with many people seeking recovery from their compulsive overeating, I can attest that those consequences, and the challenges of recovery, can feel extremely painful.

So, can a process become addictive to some people? Yes. And our next lesson will focus on one of the fastest-rising process addictions we all see in our culture today. But is everyone addicted to something? Absolutely not!

Try saying this term out loud: sex addict.

Lesson #25
YES, SEX ADDICTION IS REAL
—AND IT'S WORSE THAN
YOU MIGHT THINK

Here's a lesson that all healthcare professionals, especially therapists, need to tune in to. Then again, it's something we all need to think about, especially men who spend a lot of time alone at their computers late at night and the wives who wonder what they're doing....

Try saying this term out loud: sex addict. Does the very idea make you laugh and say, "I'd like to meet one of those!" Or does it make you shudder with images of horrific sex crimes committed against children? No question, the term "sex addict" tends to provoke some kind of response in all of us. Fortunately, the recovery community has come to recognize the reality of sex addiction and responded to the growing need for help. If you know or suspect that you, or anyone you care about, or anyone you see as a patient or client has a problem with sex addiction, that person can find treatment centers that provide excellent programs as well as recovery meetings for Sex Addicts Anonymous, Sexaholics Anonymous, or Sex & Love Addicts Anonymous. (S.A.A., S.A. and S.L.A.A. are three distinct anonymous groups, similar, but each with slightly different definitions of sobriety. Check them out and see if one or more may be helpful to you or someone you know.) You can also read more about sex addiction in valuable resource books including anything by Patrick Carnes. Out of the Shadows is one of his early books and still an excellent starting point to learn about this addiction.

We could discuss sex addiction from many vantage points, including an outline of its insidious driving forces: another way to cover or soothe difficult feelings; a substitute for dealing effectively with life, especially intimate relationships, etc. We could point to the obvious harmful consequences: destroying primary relationships; the heightened risk of contracting sexually transmitted diseases; potential legal repercussions; loss of a job or professional status, etc. But for this lesson I'd like to focus on the most prevalent but often elusive aspect of sex addiction, something we know is swirling all around us but seldom stop to really think about in a serious way.

I'm talking, of course, about Internet porn. Yes, it seems like it's everywhere and that everyone is doing it, either on their computers or via video clips on their cell phones. Internet porn is a multi-billion-dollar industry. To most people, though, whether they work in health care or not, it's just a piece of everyday American reality, like TV sitcoms or reality shows. It may be an annoyance but really, it's no big deal. Internet porn doesn't really hurt anyone, right?

Wrong! It most definitely hurts the addict, and it often harms those around him. Sorry to break it to all of you men out there who weren't expecting to come across a lesson about an activity that you may consider benign. Let's see if I can explain it in a way that might cast it in a different light, both for you and for your wife or partner.

Internet porn often leads to masturbation, which produces the body's own opiates. Those are the most addicting drugs known, comparable to heroin. You want more, so you watch more porn. The more you watch, the more your brain becomes trained to sexualize everything. Your sense of humor may change; suddenly if a joke is not sexual, it is not funny to you. You begin to think provocatively about women (or men) and sexual situations at inappropriate times and places, often with inappropriate people. Your fantasies drive you back to your Internet porn to see them acted out. Your sexual satisfaction becomes more and more compelling to you every day, practically every moment.

In terms of the porn itself, as with all addictions, you get caught in the dynamic of escalation and progression. What you find stimulating now is more hard-core than it was a year ago. You continue to seek images and situations that are wilder, raunchier, and more graphic and distanced from the reality of everyday life. You want more; you crave "different." You search the porn sites to hook into some extra titillation.

What do you think is happening? The porn begins to desensitize you. It sends a distorted message about the sexual act by depicting images that are unlike most real sexual relationships. Internet porn is especially confusing for those compulsive users who are inexperienced sexually. One study places the average age of introduction to porn, Internet or otherwise, at 11. A young boy in our community recently had a suicide attempt; clearly he had serious underlying problems, but one of them was the compulsive use of Internet porn. The shame he feels is part of the desire to disappear, to stop living. You can compare Internet porn to race car driving: if a young adolescent who does not yet drive thinks "the need for speed" is what driving is all about, it becomes difficult for him to drive normally. If he expects race car driving every time he gets in his car, routine driving at safe speeds will be boring. Similarly, if porn becomes your standard for sex, normal sex will simply not meet your expectations.

Do you see where this is leading? Using porn, Internet or otherwise, reduces your capacity to build and sustain meaningful and fulfilling intimate relationships. You become shut off from the richness and fullness of life because your mind keeps fixating on those graphic images of what you believe fulfillment is all about.

You think that nobody knows what's happening in your private theater? Wrong. On some level, she knows. She gets that something is keeping you away, immersed in your own world. The tragedy is the loss of the relationship with a human being. The harm and the emotional distance between you and your partner will keep growing until you get help.

Even if you are not in an intimate relationship, people around you may know or suspect something about your porn use by how you relate to others. They see you sexualizing people and situations and are apt to back away from you. Then your loneliness and isolation increase. And even if you do attract potential relationship and sexual partners, you may well discover how erectile dysfunction, impotence, and loss of libido are common consequences of Internet porn addiction. Those unreal expectations often lead to an inability to have real sex with a real person. Don't believe me? Google "porn, erectile dysfunction" and go to a forum to read personal accounts of impotence following regular Internet porn use. Example: Twenty-five year old man, masturbating regularly to Internet porn, meets new girlfriend, cannot perform sexually with her. Twenty-five!

Look, emotional intimacy is hard enough as it is, for any of us. Allowing another person into our lives, not just our bedroom, is scary, risky. It makes us vulnerable. We often feel that at every turn we could be laughed at or rejected. And when we begin to open ourselves to someone and attempt to form an emotional and physical attachment, we become even more vulnerable. If you fall into Internet porn addiction, you make your capacity for real intimacy much more difficult. You may never even develop the ability to be close to another human being, or you may lose it completely. You will be destined to seek that connection only externally, with the images on the screen, where you really can't find it at all.

Seventy-seven per cent of Internet porn users are male, and 46 per cent are married (2008 numbers). How would you feel if your partner went elsewhere to seek sexual satisfaction? Your wife or partner is missing out on the benefits of an honest and emotionally present relationship. The computer has become your lover, and they know, or sense, that you are having an affair, just as much as if you were involved with another woman.

Of course, many Internet porn users turn to this addictive process out of a desire to soothe the anxiety of dealing with the scary world of intimacy, as well as other areas of anxiety in their lives. But as with any addiction, that just doesn't work for long. What does work is recovery, and as I pointed out at the start of this lesson and will repeat as many times as you need to hear it, real recovery from sex addiction is available. A while ago I shared how one recovery group is taking on this challenge in my own backyard. It's probably going on in your backyard too. Sex addicts, like those addicted to anything else, deserve help, not ridicule. While I was writing this lesson, I found it so disheartening to watch the initial public reaction to the sexually inappropriate conduct of Congressman Anthony Weiner. Here was a sex addict who needed help! The media lost an opportunity to educate the public on the disease of Sex Addiction and the possibility of treatment and recovery.

If this is the kind of help you need, go find it. If you are the spouse of someone whom you believe may have a problem with sex addiction, listen to what you know. And if you are a therapist or doctor with a patient whom you suspect is addicted to Internet porn, please take the problem seriously. You will probably have to ask the question to make the diagnosis, as few sex addicts volunteer the information. It's a question well worth asking.

In case you've missed it, in many parts of the country there's a new "hot" drug out there—one currently responsible for more serious abuse than heroin or cocaine. It's methamphetamine…Speed.

Lesson #26
DRUG NEWS UPDATE:
METH IS HOTTER THAN HEROIN
OR COCAINE

Doctors often are slow to recognize addiction because they are a step behind the latest trends in the usage of harmful drugs. Here's one:

Wonder why your significant other, family member, friend, or patient is suddenly behaving erratically? They seem to be angry half the time, and they're either not around, or they're sleeping or acting strangely the rest of the time. You've wondered about alcohol but you know he doesn't drink. Have you considered the possibility of other drug use, even if you can't imagine him shooting heroin or free-basing cocaine? In case you've missed it, in many parts of the country there's a new "hot" drug out there—one currently responsible for more serious abuse than heroin or cocaine. It's methamphetamine...Speed.

Tough to live with, very tough to kick and almost impossible to use occasionally, meth has been around since the late 1800s. It was used openly during World War II (airmen's or tank chocolate) and popped up in various forms in the drug-crazed '60s. Out here where I live in the old Wild West, and most likely in your neighborhood too, meth has made a recent resurgence. It is currently the third most used and abused drug, right after alcohol and marijuana. Addicts love it because it's cheap and easy to acquire, either to buy or to make with readily available ingredients, some of which are available behind the counter of pharmacies and many other stores. There are numerous synonyms for meth: crystal, ice, crank, etc. Performance? Meth scores big points on addicts' scorecards for its immediate gratification. It provides a rapid high, similar to cocaine, but potentially more intense depending on drug quality and route of administration. It can be snorted, smoked, eaten, or injected.

119

Now let me give you the rundown on why this hot little number brings on such utter misery. With its intense craving, meth perfectly fits the addicts' saying: "one is too many and a thousand is never enough." The damage done from meth includes extreme weight loss, as well as tooth decay (meth mouth), insomnia, anorexia, severe anxiety, cardiovascular damage (heart attacks), seizures, paranoia, crawlies (sensation of bugs under the skin), and abscesses from shooting up or scratching imaginary bugs. There's more. Besides messing with your neurochemistry, methamphetamine is toxic to your central nervous system. In other words, you risk potential mental deterioration or, as addicts call it, "brain rot." Oh, and death.

And if you try to quit, although you won't face the seizures and the other physiological symptoms of withdrawal from alcohol abuse, you most likely will deal with potentially crippling depression, anxiety, and fatigue. All drugs in this category of stimulants—meth, cocaine, even prescription Dexedrine—have the capacity to beckon their former users to return, hence the need for ongoing recovery.

One recovering freebase cocaine addict still gets a physical sensation when she just looks at a picture of stimulants, either in the form of those very tiny and innocent appearing tablets (white crosses), or that fine white powder. Now bear in mind, she has not used this or any speed for over 25 years, a quarter of a century! Speed is powerful!

Not surprisingly, many meth addicts struggle with recovery even more than those addicted to alcohol or other substances. The statistics for recovery from any drug in this category are horrible. In one study of cocaine addicts in California, only 10 per cent of those who underwent 30 days of treatment were still clean two years later. The ones who stayed clean did two things: 1) Adopted a drug-free philosophy; 2) Worked a recovery program, almost always a Twelve Step program such as Cocaine Anonymous, Narcotics Anonymous, or Alcoholics Anonymous. Any will work for recovery from addiction to any drug; you just have to WORK it! Statistics for recovery from meth addiction are not reliable, but we think they are even worse than for cocaine.

If you're a healthcare professional, did you notice what their successful recovery did not include? — Doctors treating the meth addiction with another mind-altering drug, such as Xanax or Adderall.

Benzodiazepines such as Xanax reduce anxiety, but are dangerous for addicts as they are essentially alcohol in pill form. Adderall treats the symptoms of Attention Deficit Disorder that so frequently accompany the first weeks and months of being drug free. The problem is that Adderall is speed. It is comparable to methamphetamine and addicts typically crush and snort it. Both drugs prevent the addict from learning to deal with feelings and behavior drug free. Neither drug has a place with anyone who wants to be drug free and in recovery, but both are commonly prescribed to addicts in recovery.

There simply are no such diagnoses as Xanax and Adderall deficiencies!

Later in this series of lessons, I will have more to say about healthcare professionals who are quick to hand out those "recovering" drugs, and what anyone serious about recovery deserves to know and do about that. For now, I'll just say this: if you believe that you, or someone close to you, or one of your patients may have an addiction to methamphetamine, get help.

If you can get the addict into an inpatient treatment center, do it. If not, find a meeting for Crystal Meth Anonymous or whatever Twelve Step group is available in your community and get that person to run not walk to it now, even if you physically drive him to it! Yes, I have actually taken some of my own patients to meetings. Addicts have so much fear that attending their first meeting alone may be too scary. Do whatever it takes to get them there. Today!

Is there a solution to this surge of legal opiate abuse? One answer is for the medical profession to put the brakes on the system of easy handouts. Doctors, you need to give out these prescriptions much more judiciously, and in much smaller quantities.

Lesson #27
JUST BECAUSE THEY'RE LEGAL DOESN'T MEAN THEY'RE SAFE

In our cultural dialogue about cracking down on drug use, we hear a whole lot of talk about going after "those evil drug dealers and drug pushers." Stop the supply, the argument goes, and you'll shut the valve off the usage. Well, that belief is not entirely well founded for the following two reasons.

First, addiction is a disease that can only be stopped by addicts seeking and sticking with serious, long-term recovery. When addicts are using, it doesn't matter how they get their drugs; if you cut off one supply route they will simply find another one. While not the cause of addiction, easy access does fuel it, as evidenced by the increase in obesity in cultures with an abundance of unhealthy food choices and the increase in sex addiction with the advent of Internet porn. Until there are no accessible drugs, addiction will find a way to exist. Many people spend time in prison, drug free for months or years, and then get loaded during the first hours after their release. Some women stop drinking and drugging during pregnancy, only to start again as soon as their baby is born. The disease simply does not go away because of temporary lack of supply.

Second, the image of the dirty, disgusting, alley-dwelling drug pusher is largely a myth. Most addicts get their drugs from solid, respectable looking folks. That sure was true for many of the people who supplied me with my drugs, including other doctors, friends in the entertainment industry and a world-renowned musician. More important, that disgusting-looking drug dealer image cuts against the reality behind the most easily acquired drugs being abused today. I'm talking about drugs that come into the hands of people suffering from addiction via doctors' prescriptions, and sometimes even from mothers and fathers who unwittingly maintain a supply of mind-altering and addiction-feeding drugs right in their medicine cabinet.

The drugs in question here are what are often called the "legal opiates," prescription drugs that have the same qualities as heroin. Currently, the most popular names are OxyContin, Dilaudid, Percocet and their generics. If you are not familiar with these terms now, it's time to learn them. These are commonly prescribed pain-relieving medications for acute or chronic pain, often after surgery. They are all highly addictive drugs and, as their usage has soared in the last decade, there have been movements to have them banned from the market. So far, while some tighter limits have been imposed, these drugs are still readily available legally—they are major players in many of the most serious cases of addiction that we healthcare professionals see and hear about every day. In fact, evidence suggests that there are now more drug overdoses from legal opiates than from cocaine and heroin combined! Not only that, but as of 2010 there are more deaths in the United States from drug overdoses than from traffic accidents.

In and around my tiny community, during the past year alone, I've witnessed one fatal prescription drug overdose and several others that have resulted in hospitalizations, one a probable suicide attempt and another leaving brain damage in its wake. Interestingly, as I was writing this lesson I came upon media reports about the Obama administration unveiling a plan to fight prescription drug abuse. They pointed to mounting evidence of fatal overdoses from prescription drugs exceeding the combined crack epidemic of the 1980s and black tar heroin of the 1970s. In Florida alone, an average of seven deaths caused by accidental drug overdose was reported every day. While in the airport recently I saw a news account of a physician near my former community facing more than 50 criminal counts of improperly distributing oxycodone, one of the synthetic opiates similar to heroin.

Why is all this happening? It's easier to get these drugs. Addicts don't have to deal with a street supplier, although many pushers do make these same drugs available at "mark-up" rates. Currently OxyContin goes for a dollar per milligram on the street, and some addicts go through 200 mg in a day. You can get them much cheaper from a doctor's prescription, and more and more people inclined toward addiction are finding ways to start and build their supply from doctors who don't get it when it comes to the abuse of these substances. These medical providers readily hand them out, often in much larger amounts than actually needed for the intended pain relief. There are also, of course, the doctors who have really sold out. They work in "pill mills," accepting large amounts of cash for providing scripts to anyone who can pay, spending only minutes with each "patient."

I recently treated a 21 year old woman who wound up in her local hospital emergency room after overdosing on OxyContin. This was a relapse for this patient, who confided to me that she had been to a treatment center for drug addiction previously but did not stick with her recovery program. She was working at a hotel making $60 a day, and spending all $60 on OxyContin. While I tried to steer her to Narcotics Anonymous meetings, she said she was considering returning to that same treatment center for one of its relapse programs. The fee for a two-week program for those who had relapsed was hefty: $7,000. Too bad she didn't make that choice before overdosing; the Emergency Room bill alone was $10,000. Want to hear the most jolting part of her story? She got started on her Oxy habit by stealing it from her mother!

Another former patient made a career out of going from town to town along the Colorado Front Range, making appointments with doctors and dentists, eventually acquiring enough narcotics to feed her sixty Percocet a day habit. Whew! A full-time job —and she is not a very big person.

So take heed, all you moms and dads out there. You may well be unknowingly serving as the drug supplier for your child, your child's friends, or other people who happen to be in your house and snooping around out of their addictive need and a street-savvy awareness of where they might find their next fix. Yes, people really do steal leftover Percocet or OxyContin as well as other mind-altering drugs from family members or friends. Here's how: A person who is not an addict gets a prescription for 60 OxyContin pills after surgery. They try it once or twice and say, "Yuck, this stuff makes me feel stupid." So they take Tylenol or Ibuprofen and find they can get by until the pain recedes or subsides. What happens to the rest of those pain pills? Do they throw them out? Almost never. Instead, they just keep the bottle of pills around because they cost money and "you never know when I might need them again." Do they really think they might react to it differently next time? In the meantime, the baby sitter or one of their teenage children's friends comes looking and, presto—their hands are plunging into the cookie jar.

One of my former patients, an attractive, articulate, well-dressed lady, would look for notices of open houses in her community. After she spent enough time demonstrating her sincere assessment of the home for sale, she would ask, oh so sweetly, to use the bathroom. Then she'd go raid the medicine cabinet. As she related this story to me, it was amazing how often these raids would yield a considerable stash.

Then there's the growing practice among teens of what in our community are called "rollers." A group of teenagers make a pact to rummage through their houses when their parents aren't looking and swoop up assorted prescription drugs that they figure will not be missed. They put them all in a big bowl and mix them together. Then, one by one, each teen grabs one big handful of whatever pills they happen to seize. Finally, they ingest them all, quickly. Each handful usually includes lots of these pain killers, as well as an assortment of sleeping pills, anti-anxiety medications, and even antibiotics or blood pressure medication. Some of the pills may not do them much harm, but some include enough of the heavy-duty drugs such as Xanax or OxyContin to cause respiratory depression and death. Not very likely the hospital chart or police report will include the notation: "all drugs supplied by the parents of the teenagers in question." Nor does it include the sequel: teens that got high on these drugs began or perpetuated addiction to them.

Is there a solution to this surge of legal opiate abuse? One answer is for the medical profession to put the brakes on the system of easy handouts. Doctors, you need to give out these prescriptions much more judiciously, and in much smaller quantities. Several times, after I was well into my recovery and keenly aware of the dangers for addicts like me of taking these pain-killers, I have had surgical procedures that I knew would leave me in pretty significant discomfort for a short time. Normally a prescribing doc would give 60 of those pain-killing pills after one such procedure. I did accept a prescription of Percocet, but only for six, enough to take two for the first night, then one each night for the next four nights. During the day, my discomfort was easily manageable with over-the-counter medication such as Tylenol. That's all I needed, and believe me, I'm no tough guy.

Giving out these drugs in quantities of 60 is unconscionable, except for cases like terminal cancer patients. Physicians should be getting much more training and education about these addictive painkillers in med school and continuing education programs. And they should understand that pain from surgery usually eases after a few days and can be handled by over-the-counter medications—the kind of drugs that are not mind altering.

You parents out there need to do your part too. Educate yourself, and those around you, about these little demons that may be lurking in your home. Prescription narcotics and benzodiazepines, drugs like OxyContin and Xanax are dangerous. If you have brought them into your house for any reason, no matter how legitimate initially, remember that for all practical purposes you are holding the equivalent of poison—drugs that really can kill you. If you have a gun in your house and you or your children are expecting company, you lock that gun up, right? Well, you need to do the same with these drugs. And if you have been taking them and quit before you use them all, throw the rest away. Flush them, don't throw them where they can be retrieved. If you need more, you can always get another prescription. The cost is small, compared to the cost of an addict using them. Do not inadvertently become the next drug dealer on your block!

The primary reason we addicts use any drug is to change how we feel. And as most of us have learned through a little experimentation, we can do that with any one of a number of mind or mood-altering substances.

SECTION 5: TOO MANY DRUG HANDOUTS

Lesson #28
SWITCHING DRUGS IS LIKE CHANGING SEATS ON THE TITANIC

Before we probe further into what doctors do that they shouldn't do, and what they don't do that they should do in responding to people in various stages of addiction and recovery, I'd like to present an elementary teaching about the nature of taking drugs: Anyone can stop using any drug, just by starting to use another one.

When I say "anyone," yes, I mean any addict. There's a simple way to explain this. The primary reason we addicts use any drug is to change how we feel. And as most of us have learned through a little experimentation, we can do that with any one of a number of mind or mood-altering substances.

As an addict, did you have your favorite way to get high—your "drug of choice?" And if for any reason you were unable to get that drug, or you stopping using it briefly to "prove" you weren't addicted to it, what did you do? If you're like most addicts I know, within a week, or even a day, you were probably reaching out for some other drug to provide the same result: covering your feelings. Maybe you switched from alcohol to marijuana, perhaps buying into the pot smoker's insistence that weed is not mind-altering but rather "mind-enhancing." Or maybe you got off street heroin because the cost got too high or the local supply was cut or contaminated, and you switched to the legal opiates we just discussed. Some addicts who make that change, either through a doctor's prescription or a friend's handout, fool themselves into thinking that since it's a prescription drug, it's really okay. Right! We call that DENIAL. Some addicts are more honest about using their "H" in a different form and don't hide the fact they are dissolving and shooting up the prescription pills if they find the high from eating the pill is not enough.

Here's another common switch: opiate addicts turning to benzodiazepines, such as Xanax, Klonopin, Ativan, and Valium. Well, duh, it's just a matter of time before they are using both "benzos" and opiates, and I need to tell you that "benzos" are extremely mind altering. Or an addict using mind-altering substances decides that "all I'll do is drink for a while. That should keep me out of trouble, because I'm not an alcoholic." Sure, buddy. Studies in California found that nearly 100 per cent of heroin addicts who stopped using opiates for a full year but continued drinking alcohol were drinking alcoholically and having problems related to the alcohol within that year. Another duh.

As we discussed earlier, the real problem is not the choice of drugs but the addict. We addicts are searching for something, anything, to fill that void, to change how we feel, to provide a temporary respite from people, situations, reality...life! We're reaching for some drug to help us relate not to the world around us as it is but to some alternate universe we concoct. Of course, we have no idea this is what we are doing; we just want to get loaded. When we are high, we are living life through the filter of our drugs, and in the throes of addiction we are determined to never let that lens down. We may drop our drug of choice, but not the filter it represents.

The problem is that none of that switching of drugs changes the reality that addiction is a progressive disease that can and most likely will eventually lead to overdose, suicide, or some other tragedy. The end point of abuse of any drug, whether a first or second choice, is always the same: jail, a hospital, a mental institution from frying your brain cells, a nursing home from an accident that leaves you brain damaged, or death...or recovery. In my talks on addiction and recovery I warn physicians to pay attention to helping addicts become drug free, not simply switching drugs.

I teach my addict patients that doctors usually don't know they are perpetuating addiction by simply providing another mind-altering drug in place of the one that is being stopped. Switching from one drug to another is like changing seats on the Titanic: you are going down wherever you sit, whatever your drug is. It's just a matter of time.

The goal of Phase I Recovery is not to get off one drug and get on another. It is to stop using all mind-altering drugs. Period. I am not talking about antidepressants. No one gets high on them and you cannot sell them on the streets. They deserve their own discussion, so we will visit them later.

Oh, I can hear many of you addicts, appropriately proud of your recovery and everything you've come to understand about addicts and addiction, shouting out something like, "Yes, I know all that now, even if I had to learn it the hard way. But somebody had better tell all my doctors about this whole problem of switching drugs. They are the ones prescribing some kind of substitute drug. They're the problem!" Ah, my friend, I certainly agree that doctors are very much part of the problem here. That's why we're spending this time cluing them in about this issue. Let's invite them to listen in on the next lesson.

More important, expand your awareness of this world of addiction and recovery so you can see that addiction is not one of those simple "things" that you can fix.

Lesson #29
HOW CAN YOUR DOCTOR
REALLY BE YOUR PUSHER?

Doctors are used to fixing things. They figure out what's wrong with you and come up with some kind of answer to make it better. Sadly, that answer is almost always a drug. Meanwhile, addicts carry a mindset that the answer to all their problems in life can be found in...drugs. Does anyone detect the signs of a perfect storm here? Unfortunately, that's exactly what happens when addict meets doctor, and the battered bodies and minds that all too often emerge from the wreckage leave us saddened and bewildered.

Prescription drug abuse is certainly a major part of the damage. Getting hooked on prescription drugs can be the starting point for a long trail of addiction that's very difficult to turn away from, or it can serve as another source of perpetuating addiction for those addicts who have not committed to recovery. Addicts all too easily obtain prescriptions for dangerous, mind-altering drugs because addicts are very good at conning doctors, and doctors are all too good at allowing themselves to be manipulated. When doctors see or hear about any pain, physical or emotional, they've got a pill—or usually any one or more of dozens of pills—ready to combat it. And the addict, in unspoken words, says thank you very much for giving me something to deal with the emotional pain that I can't handle. That's where your doctor becomes your pusher. He fails to recognize that drugs alone can't fully heal your pain.

I present educational programs to hospital staffs and medical societies titled "Your Doctor, Your Pusher," in which I bring out a panel of addicts in recovery who testify to how easily and often they scammed doctors to get their drugs. Suffice to say, it's an eye-opening experience for many healthcare professionals. "You must think we're real pushovers, don't you?" one doc asked the panel of addicts, and they all answered, "Yeah!"

Prescribing Drugs to Addicts in Recovery

So far we've been discussing ways in which doctors who too readily hand out pain killers can trigger addiction for often unsuspecting patients or perpetuate addiction for addicts not yet committed to recovery who are using the doctor to maintain their supply. There's another tragic side to this picture of your doctor becoming your "pusher." Many times addicts who have claimed recovery and are seeking to be truly drug free run into doctors who hold a picture of recovery that still has some kind of medication in the middle of it. As we discussed in Phase I Recovery, when you are early in recovery, just days, weeks or a few months off drugs, it can feel as if you've been set adrift on an emotional river you know little or nothing about. For many addicts in this state, it's natural to turn to doctors to help provide some direction. And those doctors, the vast majority of the time, are going to escort the recovering addicts to…more drugs!

Sadly, some doctors and therapists subscribe to this guiding philosophy for treating addicts in recovery: "You can live a normal life on medication as soon as you get off these drugs!" So they load you up with benzodiazepines such as Xanax, Valium, Ativan, or Klonopin—alcohol in pill form. They are keeping you in the fog. They're just giving you tranquilizers, sedatives for your emotional pain, not diagnosing the injury to your emotional and spiritual health. And they are making a big mistake.

From my perspective of treating and being around thousands of addicts, it's absolutely clear that sedative-hypnotic medication is not the ongoing treatment for alcoholism and drug addiction. (A quick disclaimer: notice the key word ongoing in my position about using drugs for addicts. I'm not talking about the acute physical need for some medication during a brief detox period, or reasonable treatment with narcotics for severe acute pain associated with surgery or serious injury, something I'll address in a later lesson.) Conversely, abstinence from mind-altering drugs of any kind allows a recovering addict the opportunity to feel, to deal with the underlying emotional and spiritual injury that makes them think they need medication to heal.

To be clear, I am not talking about antidepressants, antibiotics, or ibuprofen. I'm talking about the benzodiazepines that we just discussed. These are the common substitute drugs that while potentially effective at keeping the addict from reaching for alcohol or their other previous drugs of choice are totally ineffective at guiding an addict to the kind of physical, emotional, and spiritual health that will sustain and nurture him or her.

People who don't work in the healthcare professions frequently ask me why doctors routinely prescribe so many addictive drugs. They just can't understand how a trained physician could give repeated, ongoing, large doses of drugs that are used primarily to get high, to zone out, or to maintain a drug habit. Believe me, they're not the only ones wondering. Hospital staff and assistants in physicians' offices often roll their eyes when they talk about the over-prescribing they see every day from their own physician employers and other providers in hospital settings. Why would any healthcare professional with a license to prescribe controlled substances hand out substances that do so much harm, even when they know they are dealing with an addict?

I ask that question all the time, and since I really do trust that most doctors are generally well meaning, the answer that I keep coming back to is this: Doctors just do not know that they are doing harm and perpetuating addiction. And they don't know what else to do. Recovery is not taught in medical school. There is no basic training in addiction and recovery early on, and then doctors head for their specializations. Even if they happen to go into psychiatry, dealing with addiction is very much medication based. They are not taught how to help patients deal with issues and make real change. Even a preponderance of non-medical therapists believes they must treat addicts with medication.

So if you are a doc who may be a player in maintaining this destructive pattern, or if you are a colleague or patient of someone you know to be over-prescribing, my hope is that you will share this information and become a part of reversing the trend. Understand that OxyContin and Percocet are the equivalent of synthetic heroin. Recognize that Klonopin and other benzos really are alcohol in pill form. Know that any addict can stop drinking when they take a benzodiazepine because they are using a substitute, but that doesn't

135

mean they are actually treating their addiction. Addiction is a disease. Xanax deficiency is not a disease.

More important, expand your awareness of this world of addiction and recovery so you can see that addiction is not one of those simple "things" that you can fix. As we've already explored in Phase I Recovery and will expand on in Phase II Recovery, this journey out of addiction is long-term, complicated, and multidimensional. Addicts are cleansing their bodies, rewiring their brains, and driving down many unknown alleys of emotional and spiritual exploration. They also have a golden opportunity to reroute themselves in a direction that can lead to inspiring views and gratifying states of being. They need extensive and intensive help from many people and forces, including those experts who can most ably guide them. This usually eliminates those who happen to have medical degrees. What addicts don't need are more drugs.

Lesson #30
BE AWARE OF "EATING" YOUR ALCOHOL

So, too many doctors give far too many drugs to addicts seeking recovery. We're working on that one. But while we do, let's not lose sight of the simple fact that there are two partners on this dance floor of addicts being given drugs: the prescribing doctors and the receiving addict. That's you! Just because your doc either doesn't know or isn't telling you the harm that drugs like Xanax can cause, at any time, but especially during the fragile period of your first year or two in recovery, doesn't mean that you can't learn what you need to know yourself. So listen closely, all you addicts seeking to sustain your Phase I Recovery.

Xanax is a mind-altering drug. Its effects on your brain chemistry are similar to alcohol. By altering your body's own neurochemicals, it makes your brain fuzzy. Even when you want to think as clearly as you can to make sense of your new world in recovery, your highest brain function is dulled. Side effects of Xanax and all drugs in the benzodiazepine category include: loss of balance and memory, inability to focus, fatigue, irritability, and more. Because these drugs are extremely mind altering and work by changing brain chemistry, they are highly addictive to individuals susceptible to addiction. The withdrawal from them, depending on how long and how much you have been using and how rapidly you discontinue, produces sweating, rapid heart rate, severe anxiety, depression, nausea, vomiting, diarrhea, and sometimes seizures. Among the saddest and most frustrating of cases I see are those where someone has been taking Xanax or something comparable for years, gets into trouble emotionally and mentally, and is then switched to another benzo, usually Klonopin. From the frying pan into the fire! There is no difference, folks. The saying that applies here is: a drug is a drug is a drug! Yes, you can be drug free, but you have to do it. You doctor probably will not.

So just because your doc tells you there are good reasons for you to take a drug like Xanax to keep you from taking the "real drugs" doesn't mean that you have to agree to take it. You don't even have to put yourself in the position of getting the offer to take it. Just as you would not walk into a barber shop if you didn't want a haircut, you may not want to visit your doctor to complain about feeling anxious while riding the turbulent waves of Phase I Recovery; you may get a haircut, or a prescription for a dangerous drug that will be the start of a relapse.

Even with all those harmful physical effects there's an even bigger reason to stay off those substitute drugs. They will impair your emotional and spiritual growth. Simply put, if you're "eating your alcohol" then you're not available for spiritual growth. If you are popping these prescribed pills any time you experience an uncomfortable feeling such as fear, anxiety, anger, or frustration, you might as well be pouring yourself a drink. It's the same thing—another way of avoiding what your body and spirit are really craving, another way of attempting to fill the void with something that does not work.

Recovery programs teach reliance on a Higher Power. If you are relying on your little helper in a bottle, whether liquid or pill, you don't get to access and use spiritual help. You are blocking the pathway that leads to understanding who you are and the possibilities life offers. You don't get to feel all your feelings when you are using drugs. Get it?

So you get to choose: spirituality or drugs. No matter what your doc knows or doesn't know about prescribing drugs to "aid" addiction recovery, you can arm yourself with the shield of your own knowledge. Do not let Xanax and the others cut you off from the Sunlight of the Spirit.

Lesson #31
WHEN YOUR DOC SELLS YOU A SECOND DIAGNOSIS, DON'T BUY IT

The mind-altering "substitute" drugs for addiction that we've been talking about often are handed out by doctors as treatment for a second diagnosis. Whether or not they acknowledge that you have an addiction, well-meaning but misinformed doctors will often diagnose you with: an anxiety disorder; ADD; obsessive-compulsive disease; bipolar disorder; etc. To them, that second diagnosis justifies prescribing the likes of Xanax, Adderall, or other comparable and mind-altering "medications" (read: drugs), all of which will keep you addicted and undermine your recovery.

Yes, these diagnoses do exist, but garden-variety addicts look like they have all of them at one time or another. Most addicts find that if they give recovery some time and attention, the appearance of other diagnoses disappears. Given a choice, the diagnosis of addiction is a great one to have. Treatment? Stay clean and sober, avoiding all mind-altering drugs, and work a Twelve Step program.

Look, I know it's hard to resist those other diagnoses. The doc or other healthcare professional describes the condition named by the second diagnosis, and it certainly sounds like what you're experiencing, right? Doctors say, "Well, as long as you're not drinking, you need something for your anxiety." So they give you Librium or Xanax on an ongoing basis, not recognizing that addicts internally live by the creed "if one is good, ten, or a hundred, is better," leading them to abuse the medication, as well as staying hooked on it. The following dialogue I had with one of my patients, about three months drug free and in recovery, working as hard as she could to stay clean, illustrates this issue:

Sara: Every time I see my therapist, she thinks I'm crazy. I feel worse. Then she sends me to see the psychiatrist and he tries to put me on something I used to abuse.

Dr. Dawn: So tell me about feeling crazy.

Sara: Well, I feel different from other people, just different.

Dr. Dawn: So what's so crazy about that? All druggies feel different when we are getting clean. It is different to be clean. We're used to being loaded, or at least high.

Sara: Sometimes I think about hurting my child. I wouldn't do it, but I have the thoughts.

Dr. Dawn: That's normal. All mothers are vulnerable, many have thoughts about hurting their kids, and since you went from the coma of drug addiction to parent, what do you expect? Yes, you need a safety net, a sure thing to not hurt him, but don't be so hard on yourself. Here's what happens when we become parents: our own childhood is in our faces and in our throats. Whatever happened to us at a specific age is brought up again when our children reach that age.

Sara: That makes sense. Johnny is almost two and that is the age when I was taken away from my parents and sent to live with relatives. I don't know what happened that my brother and I were removed, and no one will tell me.

Dr. Dawn: You have lots to be angry about. Trying to suppress anger makes us more crazy and depressed. Here are some ideas to deal with the anger when you are aware of it: write; journal about everything; go to the river and throw rocks in, hard; or go to your back yard and throw rocks...not to hurt anyone or anything, just to discharge anger. It works, it really does. Call someone in your recovery circle. Read some of the recovery literature. Do something to get through five minutes, then another five minutes. You will not continue to feel crazy, I promise. Sara, you are not crazy, you are just a garden-variety addict in early recovery.

Sara: But my therapist and psychiatrist have made lots of diagnoses of me. It changes every time I go in. They have labeled me with bipolar disease, ADD, anxiety disorder, insomnia, depression, and more I cannot remember. They want me to take medication. They prescribe Xanax, which I abused, or Adderall, which I used to snort, or Ritalin, same deal. They think I am crazy and every time I leave there I feel like there is something really wrong with me that can never be fixed.

Dr. Dawn: Well, who wouldn't be anxious, depressed, distracted, and up and down when you're coming clean into the world for the first time? You have been using mind-altering drugs for years. When you first stop, life looks scary, anxiety provoking, distracting, and up and down. That's just the way it is. You do not need new and different drugs to get through it!

Sara: But what if I really am one of those things they tell me I am?

Dr. Dawn: Look, Sara, here's the deal. Your job as a recovering addict is to allow your brain chemistry to equilibrate so we, any of us healthcare professionals, really know what you look like off drugs. Only then can we make an accurate diagnosis of any condition you really might have other than being an addict. And there's a pretty good chance there won't be any....

So that's what I tell most of the Sara's that I see, and the doctors who are choosing how to treat all the Sara's of the community of addicts in recovery. It just takes a while, six months to a year, for your neurochemistry to move towards normal. Studies show that brain function continues to recover for up to 12 months after the last use, particularly for prescription drugs like the benzos: Xanax, Valium, Librium, etc. If you are a doc or know a doc who doesn't want patients to go six hours without using something, let alone six months, it's time to catch up with what we know about recovery from addiction. Hold off on that other diagnosis. Stop your hand from scribbling the script. Let's break this down into one specific and very common diagnosis slapped on addicts in recovery: bipolar disorder, which is on the same continuum as the mood and mental disorders cyclothymia and manic-depressive disease. Remember that normal people have good days and bad days to some extent, and even good moments and bad moments. Addicts, however, have medicated these normal feelings of up and down, or sadness and joy, for many years. So when you take away their main drug, they are just not used to feeling sad, angry, etc. They say, "Oh, look at me, I'm feeling angry all the time. Something is wrong with me" or "Look how sad I am, crying half the time. Something must be wrong with me."

Doctors, rather than reflexively diagnosing these people as bipolar, consider that what you're really seeing is emotionally comparable to an adolescent, in terms of maturity, someone who just hasn't learned about the regular ups and downs of life. I understand that this desire to fix with medication is not a malicious tendency among physicians, therapists, and other healthcare providers. It's just misguided. (The mindset is found in the 1980's song by Huey Lewis, "I Want a New Drug") With an eye toward getting patients through an acute crisis, doctors don't look ahead very far. They just want to help the patient get through that worst period. They don't have the experience to know that recovery is a long, intricate process. They don't know what's possible, and they're not attuned to just how important it is to have a brain free of all drugs to move toward real physical, emotional, and spiritual health. So we'll just keep teaching them, okay?

The other piece here is that most doctors, including me, are codependent. How else could we listen to other people's problems all day? Codependents feel good when we please others, and patients are happy when we give them scripts to "fix" them. They are not so happy when we tell them to go fix themselves in Twelve Step meetings with other addicts. That's an unhappiness all of us just have to live with sometimes—if we want what's best for our patients. The truth is that we doctors cannot always fix the problem. Maybe addiction is not a medical disease; maybe it's a spiritual disease, and the cure is not found in a medical office. Hmmm.

Lesson #32
DRUGS ARE FOR DETOX, NOT FOR LIFE

Time to address the chorus that I suspect has been singing or shouting out, "But what about the need for drugs to detox? Dr. Dawn, are you really recommending having patients suffer all the terrible symptoms of withdrawal without medical help?"

Take a breath. If you're a doc who routinely assists addicts in a hospital or clinical setting immediately after they hit rock bottom, or you're a recovering addict who remembers the horrors of withdrawal and the relief you found from medication in those first few days, rest assured that I recognize and endorse the appropriate usage of medication for safe detox.

Withdrawal from alcohol and other mind-altering or addictive substances induces shaky, tearful, and painful times. There's no getting around this reality. When withdrawal is compulsory and sudden, as in behind bars or due to drying up of supplies, there is minimal help for safe detox or for the roller coaster of feelings evoked by getting clean. Depending on the duration, type, and quantity of drugs used, along with a variety of other factors, medical detox is sometimes necessary. No question. To avoid convulsions from colliding nerves, suddenly bereft of their constant infusion of drugs, medications such as Librium, Valium, or Ativan may well be the right choice—for a limited period of time. The shattered nerves that result from sudden withdrawal from certain mind and mood-altering drugs and the change in neurochemistry and shock to human physiology can be deadly, especially in the initial 48 to 72 hours after addicts have taken their last drug. The benzodiazepines, which do essentially the same thing as alcohol to our nervous system, can be life-saving when used in gradually decreasing doses to ease the process of withdrawal within that window of time.

The distinction I've been making is the difference between drugs for detox and drugs for life, or at least for those next critical months when the recovering addict will be finding their way in the world. Once a safe detox is accomplished, actually even during detox, addicts need empathy and encouragement to begin, just begin, to absorb what recovery has to offer them. After getting a patient through detox, doctors should put away the drugs. Instead of setting up a treatment plan to medicate indefinitely, they should urge that patient to go sit in meetings with other addicts who have been just where she is, and let her know that if she is willing to do what they did to get and stay clean, she has a chance for a new life and all the gifts that come with it. In other words, it's time for her to get some help from the "real" experts.

Section 6: Tuning In To the Underground

Lesson #33
THE "REAL" EXPERTS ARE THOSE WHO KNOW HOW NOT TO USE

When we've just learned that we've got any serious medical problem, we all want to find the leading experts to help us. In that search for the right person, the one who really knows his stuff and has the track record of success to call upon, we don't tend to worry a whole lot about that expert's race, religion, politics, or physical appearance. I mean, if you have a broken leg and the best orthopedic surgeon in town happens to belong to a political group or religion different from yours, or their ethnic and racial background is not the same as most of your friends and peers, would you still allow him to help you? I hope so. And yet, from what I see and hear, many addicts seeking recovery, and far too many healthcare professionals in position to guide them, steer away from the most proven experts in the field of addiction and recovery.

Why? Because judgments and prejudices blind them to the reality of who the experts really are and how much they have to offer. Whether they say it directly or just hold it as an unspoken belief, many healthcare providers and addicts themselves carry images of the majority of attendees at AA, NA, and other recovery group meetings as too rough, too unsavory, too wasted, too lost, too poor, too uneducated…too something to really provide clear, valuable, practical, proven, effective help for an addict in dire need.

Boy, talk about twisted thinking! How could anyone who really wants recovery turn away from the true experts in the field because of hair color or style, socioeconomic background, past behavior, politics, or ethnicity? First of all, those who regard the followers of AA and NA in this light are trapped in a stereotype that denies reality. The women and men who regularly attend meetings come from all backgrounds, income levels, and professions. Addiction is an equal opportunity disease. More important, those who stay away from recovery circles because "those people just don't look like me and couldn't relate to me" are missing the truth that these are the very people who have taken major strides away from the destruction of addiction and toward healthy and productive lives. Isn't that what you want to do? So repeat after me:

The real experts in addiction and recovery are those who know how not to drink or use.

Unlike treatment for a broken leg, or appendicitis, or strep throat, there is no surgical procedure or medication to cure addiction...but there IS recovery. And that's what recovering addicts who regularly and consistently show up at recovery meetings have the most experience in. Recovering addicts are not necessarily experts in anything else—although they may be talented musicians or athletes, famous authors, well respected lawyers, clergy, educators, nurses, physicians, or very good garbage collectors or housekeepers, etc.—but they know how to not use drugs. And if you or your patient wants to learn how to live life drug free, keep in mind that recovering addicts are ever willing to share their experiences and hope for a new direction.

Here's one applicable truth often told to newly clean addicts by old-timers with many years of recovery: "If you want we have, you have to do what we did." Translation: if you want the peace of long-term recovery, you have to do the work. When you're seeking to maintain Phase I Recovery, you can learn more from one person who has done what you seek to do than from dozens of others who may look like they are experts in the field but who lack the life experience to provide the most useful information and guidance.

There are hundreds of thousands of recovering men and women who are never seen by therapists, counselors, and doctors because they recover without the help of these professionals. They stop using drugs with the support and encouragement of those "others" they meet in the "underground" organizations of anonymous groups that gather in almost every country of the world.

From all my years of attending meetings in diverse towns, cities, and neighborhoods, as well as in many countries worldwide, I've been struck by how recovering addicts so effectively tear down the walls that may separate us because of our different backgrounds. I see and hear stories all the time about individuals removing campaign buttons before entering Twelve Step meetings or the refusal of attendees to discuss religion or other volatile subjects while in support groups. They are there because they take their recovery seriously. Healing from addiction is about healing from addiction. Period. They adhere to the tenth of the twelve traditions of Alcoholics Anonymous (long form) with its specific warning that "no A.A. group... should ever express an opinion on outside controversial issues, particularly those of politics, alcohol reform, or sectarian religion. The A.A. groups oppose no one." They know how to focus on the real issue, putting aside their prejudice and judgment and making room to accept personal differences. After all, once they begin to share their experiences of drinking and drugging, and the joys and challenges of recovery, they soon find that they have far more in common than any physical or superficial difference.

The longer we spend in a recovery community, the more we come to appreciate that we addicts are certainly not clones. Our clothes, hairstyles, accents, and vocabulary confirm that. I am friends with educated, articulate, older women and young, husky, motorcycle-riding, tattooed guys. Yet, we are all alike in many more ways than we are different. We are especially alike in our disease of addiction...and even more alike in our recovery. When we go to meetings, we hear our story told by someone else whose addiction is just like ours. We just have to change the name, place, or face to find the bond. And when we are sharing our joy of recovery, we melt into one mosaic of beauty and hope.

For doctors, hailing recovering addicts as the real experts in the field requires putting aside another "little" bias—the deep-seated conviction that as doctors, they are the experts on any kind of physical, psychological, or emotional problem. They are the ones who know how to fix what's wrong with patients. Many doctors somehow cling to this notion without ever having stepped foot in a recovery meeting. I'll have more to say about that problem and what can be done about it a couple of lessons later.

This is where you as a recovering addict can help. If you have begun to attend meetings, and have been soaking up the wealth of experiences and insights from those who attend, tell your doc just how valuable that input has been to you. Even if you had seen a doc previously who didn't recognize and validate the experts in the field of addiction, pay a courtesy call to update him or her on what you have come to understand. Doing your part for medical education really is part of your amend step. Since the word "amend" means to change, instead of going to your doc to get something, consider giving a bit of education. Of course, it will help to do it in nonjudgmental language and attitude, perhaps in a brief "update on my health" letter, if not in person.

Continue to trust your own eyes and ears that confirm the identity of the true experts of addiction: the ones with all the different colors and backgrounds who get together in meetings by day and night to openly share their expertise.

Lesson #34
THOSE MEETINGS ARE
YOUR MEDICINE

Okay, maybe you are a well-meaning doc or therapist, and you understand enough about addiction to recognize that recovery meetings are vital to the success of your patient. But you find that your patient pooh-poohs meetings, not only because of how the people who go there look but also because of how the meetings are run, or because of "all that religious talk." Do not make the mistake of letting the idea of meetings fall by the wayside and quickly shift to another approach that your patient will accept and commit to. Do not let that patient off the hook!

This is where you as a doc or therapist can appropriately utilize any views your patient holds of you as the expert, the voice of authority, the one who can fix their problem, the master with the magic bag to cure all ills. You can look your patient right in the eye and, with a firm but respectful manner and voice, issue the following professional decree:

"Those meetings are your medicine—you need to take it to get well!"

If you're looking for the kinder, gentler, and more fleshed out explanation, try something like this: "I respect your thoughts and opinions regarding what you have heard about or have seen regarding these recovery meetings, but you need to understand that I'm not sending you there for entertainment or conversion. I'm sending you there to save your life! If you don't want to go, or keep going, your problems are far more likely to get worse. This is part of your treatment. It's that simple."

Of course, it also helps if you have at your fingertips the literature and materials to back up your proclamations. That's why I advise the doctors I consult with about addiction to keep a current list of recovery meetings in their communities right in their office. If possible, also keep a list of individuals in recovery who can be contacted to take someone to their first meeting. As a physician, you should be just as prepared to hand out that information as you would to hand out pamphlets or brochures, or website addresses, where a patient can learn more information about any other condition you have just diagnosed.

Most patients with any physical problem feel comforted when they learn that there are others out there who know what they are experiencing or are about to undergo. Cancer patients seek out other cancer patients. Cardiac patients benefit from the stories of other cardiac patients. Those with a diagnosis that may be foreign to them are always eager to find someone else who knows what it is and has had to face it.

So you can tell your patient who happens to have the disease of addiction, and is looking at the hard road of recovery, that when they attend these meetings, they get to just sit and listen to those walking the same path tell them all about it. And be ready to point out what, to many addicts, is a vital part about this "medicine"—it's free!

Lesson #35
TAKE YOUR DOCTOR
TO A MEETING TONIGHT

One of my favorite experiences in educating other doctors about addiction and recovery emerged while teaching a group of psychiatrists in an Addiction Fellowship program at the University of Colorado. As part of the program, I got to escort them all to Twelve Step meetings. One group of three doctors, having already finished their residency in psychiatry, joined me for an inner city, Thursday evening candlelight meeting. I had approached the regular attendees beforehand to share my students' concerns that we would be intruding on them. "Of course not," the meeting regulars assured me. "We want them to see what we do here. And tell them they can stay after the meeting and we'll happily answer any of their questions." Just from watching my students during what was for each of them a first taste of recovery meetings, I knew this had been a real eye-opener. That was confirmed when we all reconvened in my office to process their experience.

"That was incredible!" one woman psychiatrist gushed. "I can't provide this."

A male psychiatrist offered his enthusiastic response in witnessing one of the women attendees. "She's so articulate, she could be a writer someday," he said. "Actually," I said, "she is a writer for a local newspaper." Others in attendance at that meeting included a nurse, a realtor, several housewives, and a good cross-section of society in general.

Again, it was so gratifying for me to witness psychiatrists coming to understand the value of what unfolds at recovery meetings, and the incredible people who have so much to offer other recovering addicts there. After hearing so many stories of the behavior of addicts from the time of their active addiction, these medical professionals were going to be far better prepared to recognize and diagnose addiction when they saw it in their patients. They would know that when it comes to the signs of addiction, if it looks like a duck, quacks like a duck, and walks like a duck, it is a duck.

"Every physician should go to some of these meetings," another psychiatrist urged.

I couldn't agree more. Going to a recovery meeting should be mandatory for every physician in training. I was reminded of this need recently when I was called by a newly appointed CEO of a small-town hospital seeking my help in educating his staff of physicians about addiction and recovery. Seems there had been a little incident at the hospital recently. When an orthopedic surgeon met with an older patient to prep him for hip replacement surgery, his patient told him that he would routinely relieve stress in his life by drinking "four or five beers" every night. So this surgeon's post-operative treatment plan included having his patient take those four or five beers while in the hospital. Surprise! That patient was typical in that he had lied about the amount of his daily drinking. The prescribed amount was a fraction of his usual routine and, being under-dosed, he went into full-blown DTs (delirium tremens).

Had that surgeon ever spent time in recovery meetings, he probably would have known that when a patient tells you he drinks four or five beers a night, the first thing you need to do is double that amount, at least. Addicts lie—to everyone. And just hearing a patient casually report that kind of regular alcohol usage ought to prompt any doc's immediate follow-up questions that would make clear he was dealing with an addict and set up an appropriate post-surgical plan. Painfully, I had to admit to that CEO that what he was reporting was all too common in hospital environments everywhere. Surgeons just want to get their patient through the first night so their "carpentry" holds up. Many don't even know that addiction is a disease. I wasn't surprised when this hospital CEO told me that in the aftermath of this fiasco he had discovered that others his staff routinely prescribed alcohol for their surgical patients.

The point here is that if a patient cannot get through one or two nights without alcohol, the doctor should recognize that as a sign that alcohol may be a problem. As with other diseases, alcoholism and addiction could and should be identified by doctors even when it is out of their area of expertise. Once the doc has a hint that he may be dealing with not only a surgical problem but addiction as well, he can tell the patient what he sees, give him a professional opinion, and refer him for help. Sure, most will not accept help the first time someone confronts them, but it might plant a seed.

Any means by which a doc can gain exposure to the underground world of recovery programs should be utilized. In other words, if you are a recovering addict who does attend meetings, and you know or suspect your doc has never witnessed one, tell him or her to go and check it out. Better yet, offer to take them yourself. You can even reassure them that if they are uncomfortable about being seen there, you will be happy to explain to anyone that your doc is there in a strictly professional capacity...assisting you!

We may be healthcare professionals but we're all human beings, and this disease of addiction spares no age, gender, socioeconomic status, or career group.

Lesson #36
IF YOU'RE A DOC ENTERING RECOVERY, GET HELP FROM OTHER DOCTORS

I know that there are many doctors out there who, like me, have recovered from their own addiction. Many more are just entering recovery, and, sadly, there are countless others who are still addicted. We may be healthcare professionals but we're all human beings, and this disease of addiction spares no age, gender, socioeconomic status, or career group. I treat many doctors, and I am always heartened when a doc has made the courageous choice to do the hard work of recovery. I also recognize how critical it is for doctors to reach out to other doctors in recovery, not just because we are in the same profession and we've been where they are. There are other issues to consider, and if you are a doc in recovery, or aware that it's time for you to begin a program, you know them well.

First, we have to deal with the stigma attached to being a healthcare professional who has undermined our own health. Then we've got to rise above our unique form of denial: "I don't need help—I'm the doctor, not the patient." On another front, doctors who get caught with a drug addiction can lose their license from state medical boards governed by tight laws that do not leave them naturally inclined to support recovery.

Fortunately, there are other resources. If you're a doc in trouble with drugs and you do not already know about those resources, now's the time to learn. First, you can join International Doctors in Alcoholics Anonymous (IDAA), an organization established in 1949 and dedicated to helping doctors in any health care field recover from addiction. This group provides a major service in helping to educate doctors about Twelve Step programs, answering questions about meetings that may be especially important to them. IDAA also holds an annual four-day meeting that attracts more than 800 recovering physicians, dentists, PHD's, and other doctorate level recovering alcoholics and addicts. IDAA also maintains an extensive, updated list of doctors in recovery willing to talk to others in need. Doctors find that you can never have too many mates who also happen to be doctors!

Closer to your own home you could track down your state's impaired physician's group. You may find there are 12 step groups and/or therapy groups specifically for professionals. You could also ask for a referral to a therapist who actually knows something about addiction and recovery. We all deserve to find and use all of the tools available to build a strong recovery.

Impaired physicians groups often are not known or utilized enough. Doctors wrestle with denial like any addict, and they all too easily get caught in the trap of believing they must not let anyone know they have a problem. Because of this fear, some referrals I receive are from the spouses of the addicted physician. I remember when the wife of a doc addicted to cocaine came into my office and asked for help for her family. It took time, but her husband did eventually hit rock bottom. Several months later, I was covering the medical director of a local treatment program for a week while he was on vacation and found that one of my patients was that physician in question. He had just entered the four-week treatment program. When I met him, and could see that he was afraid of being judged, I approached him and gave him a big hug. He had made a start, and like any of you in recovery, he had been handed the opportunity to continue to choose recovery. Far from being judged, he deserved acceptance, support, and encouragement. That's what anyone seeking recovery, physician or not, needs most.

I'd like to add one more incentive for doctors beginning their own recovery. Get well for yourself, first, and for your family and loved ones too. But also vow to get well for your patients. Also, keep in mind that if you build a long-term, stable recovery, you will be in the position of helping others, including other doctors, salvage their lives and their careers. That prospect may be hazy at best today, but believe me, it can materialize.

In an earlier lesson I mentioned how the possibility of someday helping other doctors in recovery was first introduced to me. Let me re-visit that first time. It was early in my recovery, when I was still crying at every meeting and feeling lost and scared that I couldn't make it work. A big guy named Bill, one of my new friends, wrapped his arms around me after one meeting and said, "Here, I'm going to introduce you to someone who can help you." That's when I met Dee, a therapist in recovery for several years at that point. As we walked down two flights of stairs from top floor of the AA clubhouse, I kept sobbing. "What's wrong? What's the matter?" she asked. Because she seemed like a warm and caring woman, and because she was sitting in the same inner-city Denver meetings I attended with the street people and bikers mixed in with the professionals whose offices were nearby, and probably because she asked, I told her what I did for a living.

Dee just smiled and said, "Someday from that role as a doctor you're going to be enormously helpful to many people with addiction." I'll never forget those words. Little did I know at the time how right she would prove to be. Over the years I have seen Dee at parties or other events, and we share a knowing smile. Yes, I am blessed to be in position to help many people with addiction and recovery, and being able to assist other doctors gives me a special satisfaction.

Can docs who do not have direct experience with addiction and recovery change their ways when it comes to beliefs and patterns of prescribing medication for recovering addicts?

Lesson #37
EVEN DOCTORS CAN LEARN TO JUST SAY NO

Can doctors who do not have direct experience with addiction and recovery change their ways when it comes to beliefs and patterns of prescribing medication for recovering addicts? Can they be shown that when they're treating a patient in recovery from addiction, they can make different choices in addressing the need for pain relief related to other medical issues that arise? Yes, they can, especially when we who understand the dangers of recovering addicts taking any addictive medications encourage them to try a new approach. I've been fortunate enough in my role as MD Addictionist to play some part in those reconsiderations.

Not long ago I got a call from a doc in the ER of our local hospital, where I am a consultant on addiction and recovery cases. He was seeing a patient who had come in upon suffering a relapse, and he had been able to establish that she was abusing both alcohol and other drugs. As we talked, he admitted that he was inclined to simply provide her with small amounts of the drugs she was taking, not wanting to send her away empty-handed! Uh-oh. I immediately explained to him all about the popular recovery saying, "One is too many and a thousand is never enough." Sharing from my own experience, I confided that even today when I am offered one drink I politely say "no" but I could just as easily say, "You don't have enough for me." Because once an alcoholic begins to drink, it usually goes on indefinitely.

"Let me tell you exactly where and when the next recovery meetings in our area will be held," I advised. "Tell her that's what she needs to do." He was very appreciative and thanking me said, "I really don't know anything about this disease of addiction." As we hung up I felt pleased that at least one doc in an environment and situation in which the knee-jerk response is to medicate a patient in recovery, had taken the time and energy to call me for advice and had just said no to being the drug dealer. The temptation to medicate is strong because addicts who are not firm in their commitment to recovery, or perhaps are temporarily wavering, can be very convincing in presenting their condition in a way that may appear to call for medication. And believe me, I'm not spared these campaigns for drug handouts just because of my professional experience and reputation.

Ellen, a patient I was seeing, had 12 solid years of recovery behind her. She even worked in a drug treatment center, so she was highly aware of the delicate work of recovery. She was living mostly in the world of Phase II Recovery, which we will soon explore, but when she came to see me she described feeling extremely concerned about how life had gradually become boring and her energy was always low: the big-time blahs. Did she have a low thyroid, she wondered. Should she be taking an antidepressant? Antidepressants, of course, are not addictive, abusable drugs. We know this because one does not feel any effect in the 20 minutes after taking them, there is no "high", and no addict on the streets wants them. Yes, they may change some of how one feels, but they do not provide a high like benzodiazepines, narcotics, or stimulants. While I really didn't see Ellen in danger of a relapse even if I had given her some kind of medication, I sensed that she needed something other than drugs to get her back into her recovery flow. "How many meetings are you getting to?" I asked, knowing that many helpers in treatment centers only attend meetings to take their patients. "Try getting to more for the next few months. Go through the steps again, just for yourself. Sometimes we need to re-do what we have done in the past."

Ellen didn't say much, and I had a hunch she was disappointed that she'd be walking out of my office without any prescription. (Of course, the instructions I write on my prescription pads say things like "daily meetings, exercise, etc.") I also wasn't sure if she would heed my advice. Several weeks later I received a note from her. "At first I was angry with you," she admitted. "I was thinking 'Here I am, 12 years into recovery. I don't need this!' But then I started going to more meetings again just for me anyway. I feel great. That old energy and excitement about life is back! You were right."

Sometimes a doctor will be steered in the "just say no" direction by the patient he treats. I was reminded of this some time ago when I ran into my close friend Jim, a recovering narcotic addict, physician, and athlete. I had heard that Jim had recently undergone hip replacement surgery and I asked him how it went. He explained to me that before the surgery he recognized the danger of taking narcotics, the drugs he used to abuse. "I'm more afraid of relapse than the pain," Jim told his doc. He did allow an injection of Marcaine (a long-acting Novocain, not mind altering) at the site of the surgery, so he could remain comfortable for some hours after he awakened from the general anesthetic. After that medication wore off Jim stuck to his commitment to himself to use only non-mind-altering medication such as ibuprofen, not narcotics. As he related the experience to me, yes, he was in pain, but he did not "buy into it". He had made a decision that he was simply not going to use narcotics. Two weeks later he was back in the gym, recovering nicely from surgery.

I admired Jim for putting his recovery first, for being willing to tolerate short term physical pain and refusing to take anything that could sabotage his recovery. In fact, I referred some of my patients facing surgery to Jim to hear his perspective before making the decision that was best for them. I don't wish pain on anyone, but addicts need to look at the big picture. Patients can survive a short bout of pain; patients in recovery from addiction may not survive the relapse that begins with post-op drugs.

Of course, not every recovering addict will choose to ride out the pain from surgery from day one. But we doctors can still help by sharply limiting the quantity and duration of pain-killing medication we prescribe. Joanie, a recovering addict who had sinus surgery, alertly recognized that her doc was giving her a prescription for a longer duration than she would probably need, but quite long enough to undermine her recovery. Wisely, she asked a trusted friend and neighbor to hold onto the medication for her, and only bring it over when it was time to take it. After three days, Joanne threw the rest of the pills out. Then she told her doc what she did. Maybe next time he will become one more healthcare professional who says no to huge quantities of drugs for addicts.

Just be aware that recovering people are everywhere.

Lesson #38
HEALTHCARE PROVIDERS
IN RECOVERY
OFFER A REAL CONNECTION

Most therapists and physicians are trained to keep a "professional distance" from their patients. Don't let your patient know anything about yourself, they are taught. Keep all the focus on them. Don't get entangled. Many doctors approach patients with a mindset of: See me in my office and take these prescriptions I give you, and you'll get better.

Boundaries are essential in any helping profession, of course, and there may well be good reasons for doctors and therapists to limit self-disclosure with some people they see. But for many of us healthcare professionals who happen to be in our own recovery from addiction, depression, divorce, or anything else, the idea of holding back who we really are and what we have learned to keep a "proper" distance when we are treating addicts just doesn't fit. How could we keep our own experience off limits when we know our stories of struggle and vulnerability, and our lessons learned on the road to recovery, can speak to patients in a way that those who have not been there just can't? We have an opportunity to be of service in a unique way. I certainly embrace that opportunity, and as you further your commitment to your recovery you may want to consider finding helping professionals willing to meet you in that more personal place. You may discover that doctors and other healthcare professionals in recovery often work in unconventional ways. I'll give you a few snapshots of what that looks like in my own practice:

- Several years ago, when I had a busy family practice, I was seeing a new patient who came in for a minor medical problem. In taking my usual detailed drug and alcohol history, it became clear he had addiction problem as well as a sore throat. I immediately thought of one of my ongoing patients who had

163

many years of recovery and was in the office that day for his own minor medical issue. "Let's get these two together," I said to myself. "That could provide a great initial boost for my new patient and allow my other patient to be of service, which would be a boost to him as well." So, after gaining permission from both parties, I arranged for these two patients to visit in one of my examination rooms. It worked out great for both of them, as well as for me, since I could go on to my next scheduled patients and trust these two to do what they needed to do. My new patient was grateful for this opportunity to connect with someone who understood him. My longtime patient many years in recovery appreciated the chance to share his own story.

- If I spot doctors and nurses in recovery while I am checking in with other patients in the hospital, I make eye contact, hug and ask sincerely how they are; this often becomes a 3 minute mini-meeting in a corner of the hallway.

- I once filled a receptionist position on my office staff with a woman in recovery who had been living for six months at the Salvation Army. She began to work for me the day after she got out of her six-month treatment. Staying with us for years, she continued her own recovery and was one of the best employees I ever had.

- Often my work with patients resembles more the role of therapist than physician. Ed came in wanting to talk about his disappointment over a recent visit with his brother who, like Ed, was a recovering addict. Ed hoped for real closeness but found his brother aloof, conforming to the behavior they had known growing up in a rigid, controlling environment governed by their nanny. "Remember, we addicts fear closeness," I reminded him. "But how could you have handled the situation differently to help create the kind of closeness you sought?" I guided him through a writing assignment related to the Twelve Steps to explore his role in the visit, and he left committed to changing the dynamics next time. As a healthcare professional in recovery, I am in a good position to help patients see how they got where they are in any particular problem, how their addiction plays a part in it, and how they can change. I'm always aware that there's a good chance that if they were seeing a therapist, that practitioner would know they were dealing with an addict and likely send them right to their clinical supervisor—some psychiatrist who would say, "Oh, you have anxiety? Take Xanax."

- Long ago as doctor friend acknowledged his alcoholism and entered a treatment center. He asked me to cover for his patients. His instructions to his staff on handling patient inquiries sounded something like this: "Just tell them I drink too much, I'm going into a hospital for a month to do something about it, and they should call Obrecht."

- When I give talks about addiction and recovery, whether in high schools, medical schools, or other forums, I've come to expect that after I step down from the podium I will be approached by someone from the audience who is now ready to begin recovery. I'm always happy to meet them right where they are, human being to human being, and help them do what they need to do.

When I am meeting people in a professional capacity, whether with a patient or with staff, I make a decision and judgment call each time concerning whether to reveal anything about myself or my recovery. Much of the time it is irrelevant; patients and staff just want me to be the doctor. Only if I think it will be beneficial to them do I break my own anonymity and tell them why I understand their dilemma so well.

Just be aware that recovering people are everywhere. Use them as often and as much as you need to. You will know what kind of help and which helpers are right for you. It's just one more choice available to you.

I'm just one more voice in the broad national dialogue on addiction and recovery, but I'd sure love to see what would happen if all the institutes and research centers that study addiction poured a good chunk of their resources down a different channel.

Lesson #39
POUR RESOURCES INTO TREATMENT CENTERS, NOT WONDER DRUGS

One of my favorite sayings is, "There is no magic pill for addiction recovery, and my magic wands are on back order." Addiction is a disease without a cure. As best as we can tell, it comes sweeping into the lives of addicts for any number of reasons that include our genes, neurochemical triggers, along with family environment and assorted childhood abuses and trauma. As I often emphasize, the "why" doesn't matter, only the "what are we going to do about it now." There's no wonder drug we could have taken to prevent it from starting and no magic pill that will replace the hard work of physical, emotional, and spiritual recovery.

And yet, when men and women in recovery look around, they often see and hear contrary messages that tempt them with the fantasy of being "fixed." Almost every day I come across a new book, article in a professional journal, or email from a friend or colleague relaying news about still one more drug being promoted as the be-all and end-all for treating addiction and recovery. Major resource centers such as the National Institute on Alcohol Abuse and Alcoholism regularly study a vast assortment of drugs reputed to be effective in reducing the craving for harmful drugs. I just shake my head. I don't know whether any of the drugs being assessed really do reduce any physical cravings, but I do know that the big picture needs to take in a much broader view. Why are addicts having those cravings in the first place? It's not just a physiological response. Addicts choose to numb out because of an inability to handle emotional problems and find healthy ways to address their spiritual void. Show me the drug that's going to take care of that!

One drug in the forefront of drug addiction treatment is Suboxone, currently used by many doctors seeking to get their patients off of opiate drugs, including legal opiates like OxyContin. Doctors need special training just to be allowed to prescribe this drug. One of my patients, a heroin addict trying to get completely drug free, popped a Suboxone pill that he had been prescribed by another doc just as he sat down to our appointment. I watched his demeanor and noted that within 20 minutes he wore a funny grin and was slurring his speech. When I pointed this out to him, he admitted, "Yeah, I am a little bit high from that pill." So even if Suboxone or any other drug does block the effect of the opiate, any "good" addict will try to get higher and higher on this or whatever drug you give him. And while some addicts will do better at sticking to the prescribed usage, I believe we doctors would be selling them short if we advised them that reaching this functional level is as good as it gets in life in recovery. I also want to point out that some little problems with Suboxone include overdosing on other narcotics in an effort to get high despite its high-blocking effects. (One man had respiratory arrests on two occasions. He was resuscitated both times and has lived to tell about it.) There are also reports of those who actually say Suboxone is their drug of choice!

Another common practice of doctors treating addiction is to prescribe long-term methadone maintenance for opiate (heroin, OxyContin, etc.) addicts. Early in my recovery I met Jason, who had faced this prospect and made a different choice. He had been hooked on heroin and did successfully use prescribed methadone to get off of it. Then, after being clean from everything except methadone for about two years and doing well, he decided he wanted something more out of life. He vowed that he didn't want to remain on methadone maintenance indefinitely, never being fully 100 per cent emotionally and spiritually present; he wanted to be completely drug-free. Calling upon his recovery community for support, Jason got clean from methadone and within another year had finished getting his college degree and found a job that allows international travel. He didn't settle for "as good as it gets." He went on to Phase II Recovery and continues to thrive today, more than two decades after getting of both heroin and methadone. He is such a positive model for making this choice that I confidently refer new patients to him if another physician has told them that they will need indefinite methadone maintenance in their recovery. I should note that when I "refer" patients to others in recovery to hear their stories, I make it clear that I am not referring to professionals, just to people who can share their own experience, strength, and hope.

Sometimes doctors who do tout some kind of recovery drug are at least able to acknowledge that science is not the only answer in helping addicts stay clean and live a full and vibrant life. A few years ago I heard a talk by a doc who happened to be medical director for a treatment center. He had been prescribing Campral for his in-patients at the center and for continued use at home after discharge. As he explained it, he would instruct his patients, when taking each of the three daily doses, to pray and be thankful that they were not using alcohol and to ask their Higher Power to help them get through the day sober. Placebo effect or more?

While he was seeking to present an expanded picture, I can't help thinking that what we're seeing in the recent fervent quest among so many healthcare professionals to find an addiction wonder drug is a bunch of people looking for a better mousetrap to make bigger bucks. There may be some well-intentioned thought that goes into some of these studies and trends but my belief has not wavered: there just isn't a pill for every human woe, and if there were, we addicts would take too many of them.

I'm just one more voice in the broad national dialogue on addiction and recovery, but I'd sure love to see what would happen if all the institutes and research centers that study addiction poured a good chunk of their resources down a different channel. How about investing in dozens of new and innovative inpatient treatment centers and outpatient follow-up programs for addicts who can't afford all those treatment options that cost tens of thousands of dollars? And why not expand the educational offerings for healthcare professionals so that more of them will actually know what addiction looks like and what to do about it? I'm still imagining those med school classes that I mentioned earlier that will teach doctors how not to miss the signs of addiction.

In my practice and my personal life I am blessed to witness many people whose recovery takes them on a powerful journey to enriched and satisfying lives. Hopefully, this book and my talks can encourage more of that kind of transformation. I also know that there are countless other sincere people with addiction who could go on to have very productive lives if given the resources, treatment, and opportunity. Couldn't we all devote a little more of our time, and our money, to increasing their chances—instead of handing them a drug?

PART III

Phase II Recovery: Becoming the Person You Are Meant to Be

Then some sense begins to grow inside you that the main thrust of turbulence and vulnerability, and of fear and insecurity, has eased.

PHASE II RECOVERY:
BECOMING THE PERSON YOU ARE MEANT TO BE

I can't tell you exactly when and where Phase I Recovery ends and Phase II Recovery begins. It's not a transition that can be pinpointed by time, or a specific body of work completed. It may come six months, a year, or even three or four years into your recovery. For most addicts who are committed to their long-term recovery, the entry into Phase II is more of a feeling than a date. As an addict in recovery you are most likely aware that after the first year, you have a "clean" date anniversary, often called a "birthday", to acknowledge a full year surviving without a drink or drug. You may or may not, however, have progressed much beyond the "white-knuckling" and frequent discomfort of Phase I.

Then some sense begins to grow inside you that the main thrust of turbulence and vulnerability, and of fear and insecurity, has eased. Life, however difficult, has begun to clearly reshape itself in your identity as an addict in recovery. You're not fighting against yourself or stressing about everything in your life all the time. You start to focus your attention and energy on new goals, new choices, and new opportunities that suddenly flash up on your radar screen. Instead of being sucked back toward the past, or feeling that you could be at any moment, you feel yourself pulled forward by the prospect of…something more. Rather than looking at your life through the lens of who you are not, in a life without drugs, you begin to see a picture of who you are becoming.

Do you feel that you have already entered, or may soon be knocking on the door of the exciting new domain of Phase II Recovery? Are you seeing the potential for new directions and yearning for the guidance to help you navigate all the additional choices that lie ahead? Do you hold an image of yourself as not only the productive, responsible member of society you have become through Phase I Recovery but someone who can make even more of a contribution? Let me see how I can help. In our next series of lessons, we will explore many of the most important issues involved in trying to make your recovery not just a foundation with four walls and a roof but a dwelling that begins to look and feel like your own personal palace.

The Steps become a key part of the solution for life's puzzles, choices, and decisions.

Section 7: Staying the Course

Lesson #40
KEEP WORKING THE
TWELVE STEPS

You should know up front that growing and changing in Phase II Recovery is not all happy days and harmonious nights. In fact, it takes no less work than it took to find your way out of addiction in Phase I Recovery. Sometimes it could mean you have to work even harder. But rest assured that there are many tools, resources, and ideas that can complement your efforts. And I'm sure you know by now what the first resource is:

Keep working the Twelve Steps!

As we have been discussing all along, the Twelve Steps are not a one-time test, where you answer all the questions correctly, get your grade, and move on. They represent a day-to-day process, an ongoing commitment to this new way of life. You will be turning to different steps to solve and resolve (re-solve) everyday issues. The Steps become a key part of the solution for life's puzzles, choices, and decisions. As you consider some of the additional tips I will outline next, stick close to what has brought you this far. Keep your Twelve Steps handy.

Bear this in mind if you have recently moved, or may be contemplating a move. You take who you are with you, and you will always have the Twelve Steps.

Lesson #41
IF YOU MOVE,
BUILD A NEW RECOVERY
COMMUNITY FAST

So you've built and maintained a strong, trusted recovery community. You've got plenty of mates that you see regularly and can call upon in times of need. Then, suddenly, you find yourself moving far away. Oops. What happened to that support community? Sure, you've still got the phone, email, and all the other marvels of modern communication, but as a recovering addict who had been navigating Phase I Recovery and is now eyeing the possibilities of Phase II, you know that there is no substitute for the kind of face-to-face contact that can keep you clean, with your feet firmly on the ground. What now?

The experience of Clayton will help us understand just what needs to be done, and why. Clayton is an addict who had served time in prison, obviously for a drug-related conviction. Fortunately, Clayton got clean while behind bars. He worked the Twelve Steps, took advantage of the prison recovery community and got his feet firmly planted on the Phase I Recovery trail. Before his release, some friends he had made among those who came into prison every week to bring a Twelve Step meeting to the inmates informed him of some important statistics. Studies reveal that when prisoners sober up in prison they stay sober on the outside if they continue to work the Steps and attend meetings. In fact, for those who attended a Twelve Step meeting on the day they were released, the odds of staying clean were close to 70 percent! Of those who didn't make it a priority to find a new recovery community in their first critical days on the outside, the odds of a relapse were very high.

Clayton didn't have to think twice about this. He headed right for his first meeting hours after walking out of prison, and he stayed clean. He did more than that—he kept that mindset of building a new recovery community wherever he went as he embarked on a new lifestyle. Clayton and his wife loved to travel. Since they also loved to ski, they began coming to my community of Steamboat Springs for the winter, getting by via jobs in nearby restaurants. When winter finally passed, they would head for the beaches of California, Florida or some other interesting locale. Wherever they were living, usually a new place every three or four months, they quickly became regulars in the recovery community. In fact, they found a special pleasure in going to meetings in their "home away from home" and getting to meet new folks, with different roots, who shared this common bond of commitment to recovery. It's the same joy my husband Erik and I experience when we introduce ourselves at recovery meetings in other states, or other countries when we are traveling. We in recovery truly are a worldwide community.

More important, we are a serious-minded community that provides that foundation any of us in Phase I or Phase II Recovery need. I can't say for sure but I strongly suspect that if Clayton had not made the choice to build a new recovery community in every new place he lived during these last 10 years, he may well have relapsed. When no one knows you, it's easy to start drinking or find the local drug hangouts if you're not going to meetings instead. Clayton may even have wound up back in jail, serving time for another drug-related offense instead of relishing his time embracing his "portable" recovery community.

Bear this in mind if you have recently moved, or may be contemplating a move. You take who you are with you, and you will always have the Twelve Steps. Be sure to plug into your new community of recovery meetings and the potential friendships that may emerge from attending them. Also, seek out other new friends who are living healthy lives near your new home. Watch out for old patterns that have a habit of popping up when we think we're in a "new place," the kind of patterns that, if left unexplored and not corrected, could send you reeling closer to an old familiar place, relapse to active addiction.

Lesson #42
SAY YES TO OPPORTUNITIES
TO BOOST YOUR EMOTIONAL
AND SPIRITUAL HEALING

So you've been diligently following your recovery program: staying clean, working the Twelve Steps, going to meetings, building a community of mates to support you, staying connected with your sponsor, staying away from your old druggie pals, and even becoming more physically active. Great! But keep your eyes open. With your new ways of thinking and acting, you may now recognize opportunities in Phase II Recovery for new and often unexpected opportunities to bolster your emotional and spiritual well-being. I'll give you an example.

This happened a couple of years into my recovery, so I already had done a fair amount of emotional and spiritual work in charting new directions in my life during Phase I Recovery. I also knew I had a long way to go to claim the kind of emotional and spiritual health that I really yearned for. I was still often feeling quite depressed, and while my parenting had vastly improved I was not always patient with my daughters. These signs indicated that I had not fully resolved all my anger issues, and I really didn't want to keep dragging those chains around as I tried to move forward in new life directions.

Fortunately, I had met Mary, a therapist who was part of a team of colleagues that led three-day therapy retreats for those in recovery. In a safe, supportive environment, this team introduced us to psychodrama as a way to let go of deep, pent-up feelings. Since much of my anger was still directed at my father and mother, I was invited to have stand-ins from the group role-play each of my parents. Screaming out my anger toward them helped. I found taking the foam bat and pounding it into the floor or a pillow even more therapeutic Understand, I was in no way imagining doing physical harm to my parents. Rather, I was giving bodily, physical expression to my feelings

179

of anger toward them. It was the first time I had ever done this kind of "anger work," and I soaked it up, relishing in the sense of moving what had been in my head into my gut. I was finally able to internalize resolution of much of the pain from childhood with two alcoholic parents. I was taking the work I had done in the steps to a new dimension. Very soon after this experience, I was able to move on to forgiveness. I remain thankful to this day that I was able to forgive my parents for being exactly who they were, nothing more, nothing less; and I was able to do it before they died.

Behind the anger were lots of tears, and amid the sobs I had the experience of "saying goodbye" to my mother. No, not in the way of wanting her out of my life. Far from it...I was really saying goodbye to the kind of relationship I had known all those years with her, and my way of looking at her: the alcoholic mother who would not leave her alcoholic husband and chart out a healthy lifestyle for herself and her two children. Through this boost of emotional and spiritual healing, I was freeing up room to look at my mother in an entirely different light: a loving and caring woman who did her best with what she had to work with. What a relief!

Additional growth for me took the form of allowing a new relationship with God. As you may recall, I was one of those recovering addicts who did not initially embrace the use of the "G" word in the recovery program. Reciting the serenity prayer in meetings was acceptable, but actually saying that I believed in God and cultivating an active, ongoing relationship with Him? Not for me, at least not at first. By my second year of recovery I was actually using the "G" word voluntarily, keeping the serenity prayer on my refrigerator door, and warming up to the common recovery saying, "I don't believe in miracles; I depend on them." While I was not yet going to church, I had reached the point of opening to a real relationship with God, just allowing it to be.

As I reflect on these and other healing opportunities, which I sometimes do when I'm simply sitting in recovery meetings, even those in other countries where I do not speak the language, I hail them as major catalysts in preparing me for another major, healthy life change: meeting Erik and allowing a marriage with some really positive ingredients.

So what might be available to you for additional emotional and spiritual growth? And what may lay waiting for you on the other side? Go find out. Consider suggestions you may hear for deeper therapeutic work on issues that still trouble you. Watch for conferences or workshops that specifically address long-term changes for addicts in recovery. Several well-known AA speakers address "second stage recovery and their talks are available on CD. Keep your ear open for stories in your recovery meetings from others sharing an experience about some new endeavor that both challenged them and left them with a greater sense of peace or happiness in their Phase II Recovery. Practice the open-mindedness that you cultivated in Phase I Recovery about pursuits and experiences that can now take you to new places—places where you can really begin to soar!

Changing our past means changing how the events that unfolded affect us today, as an adult committed to the path of ongoing, Phase II Recovery.

Section 8: Changing Your Past

Lesson #43
YES, YOU CAN CHANGE YOUR PAST

"You *can't* change your past." You hear those words all the time, not only in recovery circles but also in therapists' offices, prisons, or anywhere else someone may land after going through a tough time. Sometimes the words spill out as a sour-note lament by an addict stuck in her unwillingness to take personal responsibility. The added lines usually go something like, "If only I had been born into a different family" or "If only I had married someone else" or "If only I hadn't been fired" or, among the self-deprecating, "Why did I do that?" These laments are something of a combination of complaining and denying. Often the conviction that one cannot change his past is used to continue to beat up one's self and remain in the victim role. "If I wasn't such a loser…"

Sometimes the phrase is offered more as a beginning point for acceptance and letting go for those seeking to rebuild their life. The next lines of this well-meaning chorus sound something like this: "You can't rewrite the script of what has happened to you. You need to accept the past and focus on what you can do in the present and the future." Good, solid advice, right? Well, yes…and no. We addicts certainly do need to come to grips with what has happened to us, and what we did to others and ourselves when we were using drugs. And we sure need to focus on the present—living one day at a time—as well as point ourselves toward a healthier future. That's all part of Phase I Recovery. But that part about "changing" our past? I've actually got a different view, an alternate perspective that has opened my eyes and the eyes of many patients and friends. I invite you to consider it now.

Yes, you can change your past. And doing so can provide a major boost in your emotional and spiritual growth as you explore the possibilities of Phase II Recovery.

Wait a minute; didn't I say earlier that I don't have a magic wand? How am I going to get you to wipe out all the painful, nasty business of your yesterdays? Am I suggesting that the horrors of experiences such as childhood abuse or the frightful nights with a raging alcoholic father will simply disappear from your logbook of life?

Not at all. You can't change the facts of your childhood, or the facts of your own unhealthy behavior as an active addict in adulthood. Those bad things did happen. They won't go away, can't be removed. But I've come to understand that our past and how we look at it is not essentially about facts. Nope. It's actually our sense of what happened in our past, the context and meaning we apply to it. It is the story that we tell ourselves, and anyone else who will listen, about our past. And that story really can be changed, altered, abridged, and amended. The story we used to tell can become an old movie, one that we choose not to play any longer because we have found a new movie that not only is more fun to watch but also is designed to better serve us.

We change our past by seeing it very differently than we used to. Changing our past means changing how the events that unfolded affect us today, as an adult committed to the path of ongoing, Phase II Recovery. When we change our past, we are writing that new story; a story that may include different points of emphasis; a story that we may tell with a different tone or attitude, without the complaining and denying; a story that fits who we are becoming. "We will not regret the past nor wish to shut the door on it," is a direct quote from the book, *Alcoholics Anonymous*. Truly, we do find that we could not get here, here in the joy and satisfaction found in Phase II, without going through all of our past. Surviving and thriving through past adversity magnifies that joy in the present.

As I explain how to approach this process of changing your past, you might discover that this is something you already have been doing, just by continuing to live in the steps and seeking to maintain a sturdy, consistent Phase I Recovery. Even if you have not covered any of this new ground yet, you are likely to find that it's a natural process in alignment with other recovery work you have tackled. After all, most healing journeys include some time spent on resolving our past. But let's look more closely at that word: resolve. Break it up and you have re-solve. That's what we're going to be doing—re-solving the puzzle of your past and studying the new picture that the pieces suggest. The next three lessons will show you how.

First, you will be guided into looking at what happened and how it influenced you. Then, you will be shown how tapping the courage to relive the old pain can set you free from it. Finally, you will learn of the exciting new doors that may open for you and for your loved ones when you have that new story of your past.

As addicts, as human beings, the wounds of our past do leave an indelible mark.

Lesson #44
RECOGNIZE HOW YOU DRAGGED YOUR PAST INTO YOUR PRESENT

Some years ago I was conferring with another doc about a mutual patient and the problems she was confronting. When I mentioned that she had grown up with an alcoholic, abusive father, I watched this doc frown. "Well, that's in the past," he quipped. "I don't think that has anything to do with her issues today. Its 30 years later. All of that is over. She's an adult." After picking up my jaw that had dropped to the floor when I realized how uninformed this doctor really was, I attempted to explain.

As addicts, as human beings, the wounds of our past do leave an indelible mark. They have shaped us, defined us, and fed us a string of messages about ourselves, about others, about life. When we became adults, we carried the weight of all that pain with us and frequently re-created the unhealthy behavior and destructive roles we knew growing up. We dragged our past into the present. It permeated our thinking and our acting, coloring much of our addictive lives.

Of course, we couldn't see how that was true when we were using. Once we begin walking the new path of recovery, however, we have both an opportunity and a responsibility to recognize what happened. We really do get to "re-solve" our past, and it begins with spending some time answering these three basic questions
1. What happened?
2. What did I do with it?
3. How did I drag my past into my present?

When I set out to re-solve my own past, my answers spilled out in a torrent of vivid memories and stinging emotions:

What happened? I grew up in a chaotic home with a raging alcoholic father who verbally abused my mother and, when I got a bit older, directed that verbal abuse towards me. I lived in constant fear of what he would do next. As a toddler, I begged my mother to take me to school. Did I comprehend at that early age that was one way to get out of our house? In preschool I could never fall asleep at naptime, a likely byproduct of feeling as if I had to be constantly on guard against his raging and threats. At home, I hid in the relative safety of my room whenever I could, coming out only after he had passed out again.

What did I do with it? Once I was old enough to recognize that our fear-shrouded home was not how every kid lived, I fell into shame. I swallowed a message that I was bad, different, not acceptable, undeserving of being alive. The unconscious message to myself was that if I was at all worthy, my father would not drink and rage at us and my mother would not drink and either yell back or cower from him. It was all my fault. If I was good, or even acceptable, the adults in my life would have shown love, caring, and empathy toward me. Instead, they left me in my private horror.

How did I drag my past into my present? As I reached adulthood I was weighed down with all sorts of crippling messages: "I am not good enough; the adults I depend on will hurt me; I must control everything or chaos will result; I must do things perfectly or I won't get what I need; I can't rest—life is too serious, too dangerous." So what did I do with that? Distorting this sense, I concluded that I would attempt to hold off the chaos by getting a responsible job—maybe as a doctor I could fix my parents. Early relationships were superficial and based on getting high together. The longest lasting one was with a man who demonstrated qualities familiar to me: he was critical, judgmental, and emotionally unavailable, like my father. Also, I decided (not consciously, of course) that since people who were drunk and irresponsible were familiar, I would hang out with them, and that those who were responsible, sober and emotionally present were scary, so I would avoid them. And of course I would use drugs to avoid or cover all the unwanted and overwhelming feelings.

Then, as a mother, I really dragged the chains of my past into my present. I loved my two daughters more than my very life, but I was consistently unable to remain physically and emotionally present for them and all their critical needs. I was too busy surviving my own pain. With the arrival of children, my own childhood was even more in my face, my old pain resurfacing at every stage of development, theirs and mine. I used work, alcohol, and other drugs to avoid what I could.

When I looked back at my first years of motherhood from the clarity of recovery, I was struck by the image of my oldest daughter Brie, at age 3, almost bald on one side of her head from pulling out most of her hair. She was no doubt tormented by the very same messages my parents had given me: "You are not good enough for me to pay attention to you. If you were a better daughter, I would be a better mother. You are not worthy of my time and attention; I will withdraw into my alcohol and drugs every night instead of really being there for you." I have many other painful snapshots from those vulnerable years of my daughters' childhood. These were the humbling discoveries I made when I answered those three key questions to begin re-solving my past.

How about you: what happened in your past that was difficult or painful? What did you do with it? What internal messages did you live by? How did you drag your past into your present? Retrace your steps. As best as you can, put names to the behavior and the feelings. Be honest about what you did in your active addiction that you know was a carry-over from what had been done to you. Use your journal to write down your ideas. Turn to your sponsor, therapist, or others in your recovery circle for help and support.

Remember, this process does not end here. The goal is to change your past, to enter into a new relationship with it. Far from wallowing in what happened, or blaming yourself for what you inadvertently repeated, you're moving toward a place of feeling a greater peace with your past so that your road ahead will be free of the chains that held you down. In the next lesson we will move closer toward that goal, as we uncover the next piece of the re-solving puzzle.

Fortunately, I had good friends in recovery who told me point-blank that I would need to break free from those resentments to progress in my emotional and spiritual growth.

Lesson #45
WHEN YOU RE-LIVE THE OLD PAIN, YOU SEE IT ALL IN A NEW LIGHT

When you are first finding your way in recovery, it is natural to be angry at all those who harmed you. In my first months trying to live clean, I was filled with rage toward my parents. I hated them! My head was filled with all the overwhelming evidence of just how sick and evil they were, and all those terrible things they had done to me. I could name in vivid detail everything that they had not given me. And I could have remained stuck right there. Fortunately, I had good friends in recovery who told me point-blank that I would need to break free from those resentments to progress in my emotional and spiritual growth. In other words, I needed to keep following the instructions to re-solve my past.

Earlier, I shared with you how the Twelve Steps of AA and NA were instrumental in helping me access and release those old, painful feelings. When I was writing my first attempt at the fourth step—making that fearless moral inventory—I cried and cried, awash in the memories of what been done to me, and then what I had done to those I loved in re-creating my past. A powerful workshop led by wise therapists skilled at facilitating emotional work helped me to further express and release the old pain, especially the anger. That experience opened the door to a wellspring of peace and acceptance in my life in Phase II Recovery.

So how about you? I trust that you have begun doing your own work to re-live your painful feelings from the past. I urge you to continue to find new outlets to do that, in safe and supportive environments. Recovery literature tells us to get additional help if we need it. Addicts and alcoholics almost all qualify for Al-Anon, as we all have family and friends with the disease. Al-Anon can help us detach from our destructive family dysfunction. As addicts we became all too adept at avoiding, denying, and suppressing pain, and trying to cover all our feelings with drugs. But now, in the interest of re-solving your past, try to keep your channel of feelings open. Let the old pain out until it begins to lose its grip on you. Re-live it, re-feel it, re-solve it.

How will you know when that has happened? The key signs are noticing more and more positive feelings in your day-to-day life, and a shifting perspective or attitude toward the roots of all that old pain and the circumstances around it. When I began to rewrite old messages and change old beliefs, I found that I could approach my adult life in recovery feeling far less scared. I learned that I did not need to control everything...that I was not perfect and did not have to be perfect for others to accept me... that people, maybe especially those who were clean, were usually trustworthy. I began to acquire self-acceptance, and the ability to accept and show compassion for others.

Those were enormous gifts from re-solving my past, but perhaps the greater and more unexpected gifts came in how I looked at the primary people in my past: my parents. Free of my resentments toward them, I could slowly acknowledge that they were just people who suffered the disease of alcoholism, with the classic personality traits of most addicts: self-hatred, fear, pride, anger, narrow-sightedness, stubbornness in refusing to ask for help, etc. They were just doing the best they could with what they had to work with. And there was more. As I could now see for the first time, that list did not fully define them as people. There were other sides to them, other parts to the puzzle of my past, parts that I had forgotten.

The truth was that both my mother and my father could be loving, kind, caring individuals. The evidence on this side began to mount right at my birth, or rather pre-birth. Before I came along, my mother, born in 1910 had endured three miscarriages and pioneering surgery to remove uterine fibroids. She was 38 years old. When she was told I was a breech baby, she opted for one of the first Cesarean sections done with spinal anesthetic so that she could watch my birth with a mirror. How courageous! An accomplished journalist and writer, my mother taught me how to speak English correctly, which so few people do today. She also impressed upon me that no one was better than me or less than me, an attitude that I am grateful to carry to this day. She took me to ballet classes, which led to my opportunity as an

11-year-old girl to play Clare in "The Nutcracker" with the Ballet Russe on the Lyric Stage in Baltimore. What an experience!

And look at my dad: he taught me how to swim in the ocean at age 5. As an adult, I have competed in Ironman triathlons where the 2½ mile swim takes place in the ocean. I seriously doubt I would ever have been able to do that, had I not learned as a child how to handle ocean swims. Dad built me a wonderful playhouse. He helped me plant my own strawberry patch in the garden when I was 9. And, driven by his desire to give his kids more than he had, he not only put my brother and me through college but paid for all of medical school for both of us as well. He did all that by running a dog food business, prompting my brother and me, in our lighter moments, to quip, "I got through med school on dog food." So when I finished my training and opened my first office, I was free of any debt. How amazing was that!

With these warm and poignant memories, I now had a new picture of my past, a more complete puzzle. Sure, the negative stuff was still there. But it had been changed in color and shape. I could, when necessary, bring all the nasty stuff to the forefront of my mind and describe it in a functional, non-complaining way, something I still do in my talks in recovery groups so others with painful pasts will know that I've been there too. Yes, my parents really did this and they did that, but it was the best they could do. Yet at the same time I could see these other puzzle pieces, the other dimension to the mosaic, where they were two people who did give me a great deal and loved me as much as any child was ever loved. With this more complete and balanced picture, I could choose which parts of my past I wanted to keep most prominent in my mind, and which parts I could allow to fade into the background. From then on, I could choose to tell the story of my past in a way I could never have dreamed of sharing before. I had re-written the script, and re-solved my past.

That's the fresh perspective, the new light that was revealed to me. I can't tell you what it will look like to you, but I believe it's there. Keep turning over the pieces. Scan the viewfinder of your past and pay attention to that evidence from the "other" side of the case. You'll find it.

Thank God I was given the tools to break the cycle of addiction! If you have children, do you see the beautiful ripples that you are sending them through your recovery?

Lesson #46
WHEN YOU CHANGE YOUR PAST, YOU CHANGE YOUR CHILDREN'S PAST

I have another snapshot image of myself as a mother before I chose the path of recovery and went on to do the work of re-solving my past in Phase II Recovery. Brie was 5 or 6 at the time, and as she entered the kitchen early one evening while I supposedly was focused on fixing dinner, she tried to make sense of what she was seeing. "What are you doing?" she asked innocently. What was I doing? ...Snorting cocaine, of course.

I still cringe when I imagine how the childhood of Brie and her younger sister Kara could have unfolded. Had I not been granted the gift of recovery, they would have continued to grow up in a verbally abusive, heavy drinking and drugging household, with two parents who were models of poor impulse control, irresponsibility, and constant blaming of one another. They would have learned none of the ingredients of a happy, healthy marriage: emotional intimacy, cooperation, common goals, support of individuality, negotiation, genuine caring, etc. They would have reaped none of the benefits of a functional home: unselfish love, acceptance, flexibility, and appropriate boundaries. Plain and simple, they would have been deprived of the opportunity to become the best women they could be. And when they grew up, they would have had to work twice as hard at re-solving their past with an addicted mother.

Thank God I was given the tools to break the cycle of addiction! If you have children, do you see the beautiful ripples that you are sending them through your recovery? First, and most important, you are reshaping their present by your commitment to live a clean, healthy life. Rather than harming them with your destructive behavior, you're tapping a deeper reservoir of love, caring, empathy, compassion, and responsible guidance. As you build a stronger

195

foundation for them today, you are enhancing the chances that they will thrive tomorrow. As I look back at the years of sharing my life in recovery with my daughters, I often say "we" grew up together. In witnessing my efforts to understand and practice what it meant to be a healthy, responsible adult, they were better positioned to step into their own mature adulthood. And after "we" welcomed my husband Erik into our lives, they had a model of a healthy, vibrant marriage with a mother and stepfather who loved and supported one another, took responsibility for themselves, and centered their lives on sustaining a healthy family.

That's how I came to recognize the third part of the gift of recovery to my children, the same kind of gift you may find yourself offering now. As parents, in changing our past we really are changing their past. Every grown-up must and will inevitably take inventory of their past and seek to re-solve it. Yes, my daughters' past still includes images or at least a vague sense that their mother used to be very sick and acted in totally unhealthy and inappropriate ways. The girls can use that as a distant memory of how they do not want to be. But their past also includes a whole other bank of information and experiences to draw upon: emotional health, respectful communication, honesty and love. My recovery blew up one emerging puzzle of their past and substituted a very different one. They hold wonderful pictures of childhood—and some yucky ones. They get to choose how to make sense of it all, how to re-solve their past. By following the path of recovery, I gave them a balance to consider. Isn't that a major part of what any of us as parents seek to provide?

Section 9: Conquering the Final Frontier: Relationships

Lesson #47
STEP CAREFULLY BACK INTO THE GAME

Did you botch all your personal relationships when you were using drugs? When you look back at your track record in this domain, do you see mostly a litany of dishonesty, mistrust, betrayal, jealousy, blaming, recklessness, disrespect, inconsideration, secrecy, and general unreliability? You're certainly not alone on that one! When you first attended recovery meetings you no doubt heard frighteningly similar stories from other addicts admitting to how they ruined and sabotaged their closest personal relationships.

Yes, we addicts tend to make a mess of our relationships while using drugs. Then, when we entered Phase I Recovery, we faced the daunting challenge of first trying to decipher what we did to undermine relationships with those we profess to have loved, and then somehow figure out how we're supposed to do it any differently without drugs. Twelve Step work, especially steps four through seven, helps with this painful process. For most of us, the second part of the challenge appeared impossible for much of Phase I, so we carried it over into life in Phase II Recovery. Relationships are the Final Frontier for addicts committed to living a healthy, vibrant, satisfying life.

Not always easy for normal, emotionally stable people, they are often baffling for those of us with dysfunctional role models, not to mention our inherent immaturity and selfishness. While we addicts yearn for real closeness, we also fear it. We usually enter the arena with no real models and no taste of what it means to begin and build a real relationship. We're scrambling through the dark thicket of the woods, lost without a compass.

That's why many addicts find it natural during Phase I Recovery to shy away from new relationships, or step gingerly into the task of rebuilding a marriage on the rocks from their destructive behavior. We move slowly, awkwardly. We may experiment a little, and make a lot of mistakes. We may be tempted to swear off intimate relationships altogether or at least take a long hiatus from them. More likely, we reflexively enter into a relationship with the first person who seems to understand us. Because others in recovery do understand us, it is common for addicts to become intimately involved with each other in early recovery. Oops. Pay attention to the saying that goes around Twelve Step programs: don't make any major changes during the first year clean. Specifically, no divorces or new relationships...Right? Very few adhere to this warning. Most of these relationships result in breakups in a short time, but many continue on as friendships.

It makes sense to avoid those major changes, especially with relationships, because our first mission is not only to stay clean but also to learn who we are as a person who no longer uses drugs. We human beings are attracted to our emotional equals; if one grows and the other does not, someone is left in the dust as the other outgrows him or her. Yet, as we move further into Phase II Recovery, we find that the hunger to be close to a man or woman in a loving and intimate relationship is too strong to hold at bay. We really do want to step back into the game, and we want to play it right this time.

If that is where you happen to be, or where you suspect you will be soon, I want to help you walk more fearlessly into this new frontier. In the next three lessons, you will discover or re-learn some of the material you missed in the classroom of real relationships during all those years of your addiction. If you are from an alcoholic, abusive or otherwise dysfunctional household, you missed it growing up as well. So, even if you're feeling nervous, step right in. You are definitely not alone.

Lesson #48
To Make a Healthy Relationship, You Need the Right Ingredients

Let's consider for a moment what we as addicts bring to the table in hoping to create a rich and rewarding relationship. Our brain is fried, or at least confused from years of using drugs. Hmm, that might not be so helpful. We're stuck at the maturity level of when we began to use. Well, that's not so good either, especially if we began using as a teenager or earlier. I don't know too many teens that look equipped to construct a lasting relationship, do you? Also, most of the relationships we have known, as well as those we have been a part of, were always fraught with conflict, much of it stemming from our own self-centeredness. Okay, that's not something that is especially attractive or helpful either.

Face it, as an addict in recovery with an interest in or at least a curiosity about healthy relationships, you are most likely building from the ground up. So where do you even start? Start by looking at people around you who have managed to construct a solid foundation of peace, joy, and happiness in their lives—including their relationships. How did they do it? What were the ingredients they mixed together to cook up a loving, caring, satisfying union with another human being?

Here are some of the key qualities:

- Respect
- Acceptance
- Communication
- Caring
- Kindness
- Openness

- ¤ Honesty
- ¤ Generosity
- ¤ Willingness to acknowledge mistakes and apologize when wrong
- ¤ Ability to set and maintain boundaries
- ¤ Awareness of the balance of independence and dependence
- ¤ Commitment to grow emotionally and spiritually

Feeling a bit overwhelmed? Well, I could go on. The inventory of what goes into a positive relationship makes for a very long list. But I'll stop there for now. And for this lesson, I will invite you to look more closely at just one key ingredient: communication.

Somewhere we've heard that good communication is critical in any well-functioning relationship, but when our brains were altered and we were stuck at the age of when we began using, what do we know about communication? What we do know, and were no doubt pretty darn good at, was being self-centered and preoccupied. We were good at taking things out on others when we were angry with ourselves. We were good at avoiding any communication with people we didn't want to face, or at least worming our way out of situations where we might have to talk to someone right away. When we were forced to try to communicate, we were good at making excuses, or telling lies to cover our tracks. We were good at looking sincere while communicating insincerely, and we perfected the art of assuming others knew how we felt so we wouldn't have to try to explain it. Off the hook and not taking responsibility for ourselves, we could just discount others who could not read our minds.

Is there any hope for us in learning good communication, beyond a few of the basics we discussed in the Communications 101 course in Phase I Recovery? Can we really learn to effectively communicate with another person in a successful intimate relationship? Sure we can, and here's the first step: get out of yourself. Train yourself to become more aware of the other person. Treat him or her as you would want to be treated. When you are struggling with a painful feeling such as anger or sadness, let the other person know what you are experiencing, while assuring him or her that it is not about them.

200

When the other person reaches out to communicate to you, acknowledge hearing them, even if you can't respond immediately. And when you sit down to try to communicate together, listen first and resist the urge to interrupt, judge, criticize or "should" on her or him. When you have a request or a need, state it clearly, directly, and in a timely manner. Stop blaming; grow up; take responsibility for yourself and the messages you convey to others, verbally and nonverbally. (No eye-rolling, please!)

These communication skills dramatically elevate our chances of enjoying satisfying relationships not only with a significant other but with the full circle of family, friends, colleagues, and others with whom we closely relate. And they all sound pretty simple, right? Yes, but for self-centered human beings, especially for addicts in recovery, simple does not mean easy. These skills take time, practice, and patience. But it's worth it because becoming proficient at really communicating with another person really may be that one essential ingredient that will enable you to have increasingly satisfying relationships.

Reconstructing relationships damaged by addiction can happen during recovery.

Lesson #49
WHAT IF YOUR MARRIAGE FAILS TO SUPPORT YOUR RECOVERY?

If anyone were to do a research study on recovering addicts who relapse, they would undoubtedly find that many failures are ignited by new or ongoing problems with the addict's intimate relationships. We've already explored how addicts sabotage relationships because they can't get out of themselves to really see and know their partner. At the same time they are holding back, not letting their partner know them due to fear that being truly known will lead to rejection. Root cause: "I'm not good enough. If they really know me, they will leave me." Addicts often enter recovery carrying a long history of dishonesty, cheating, blaming, and inciting fear and jealousy, not to mention being stoned and unreliable much of the time. They have exhibited behavior that tears relationships apart. Clearly, rebuilding trust in those relationships will take a great deal of time and commitment. Marriage counseling can be helpful, and the addict's personal exploration in his or her recovery program is critical.

Reconstructing relationships damaged by addiction can happen during recovery. Many addicts who are clean have learned to deal with their fear of rejection and found ways to share themselves in open and increasingly unselfish ways, accepting others as they are, encouraging growth, and sincerely wanting the best for the other person. When that happens, great! But my own experience and many examples I've seen from others' situations remind me that it may not always work out that way. Despite real effort on the part of one or both spouses during Phase I Recovery, and even onto Phase II Recovery, some marriages don't stand up to the daunting challenges of addiction and recovery. That may be especially true for an addict who is going through a recovery with a spouse who does not seem to support that recovery and declines to participate in some way. Attending meetings with an addict, or attending Al-Anon, can not only demonstrate support but can become a source of support and growth for the spouse and other family members. Some spouses recognize this, but others don't.

I'll take you back to my own marital struggles in the initial period of my recovery. First, I need to issue a disclaimer: while I will point out behavior on my husband's part that contributed to the actions I ultimately took, I take full responsibility for all my choices. Like me, my husband at that that time was just a human being doing the best he could. My shortcomings as a marital partner, and my list of misdeeds that derailed our chances of having a healthy relationship, are too numerous to count! I am simply sharing my experience at the time on the chance that it may shed light on your situation.

So, going back to my marriage and the turmoil I found myself in.... I had heard the oft-repeated belief in recovery circles that in the first three to six months of recovery you will decide if you are going to "buy" this recovery idea. Phase I Recovery is indeed a fragile, unstable time. Well, I was buying it all the way. I was attending meetings almost daily for the first three months, then three or four times a week. Think about how much recovery I was getting. Most semester-long college classes are only once or twice a week for four to six months. I was getting many times that, really rapid learning. New information, new ways of being, thinking and behaving were being offered to me every day. Growth becomes logarithmic for anyone who internalizes recovery at this level. The process is so much more than just not using substances! I understood on a gut level that I needed immersion in recovery if it was to work for me. I had spent years immersed in alcohol and drug use, almost daily. Why not put as much time and energy into my recovery as into my using? As part of that commitment, I cleaned our house of alcohol and drugs. I was doing my best at working the Twelve Steps and confronting all the emotional upheaval.

Unfortunately, my (now ex) husband was not consistently cheering me on. Once when I told him I was going out for a specific meeting in our town, he said, "Wait, you just went to that one last week." I shared with you how, when we visited his parents, he wanted me to hide the fact that I had stopped drinking and had begun a recovery program. After I finally revealed my addiction to his parents, we argued about it in the car. He still didn't think what I did was appropriate. I knew, however, that I needed to be honest with my family, including my in-laws. I was beginning to understand the recovery saying, "you are just as sick are your secrets," and did not want to hide something as important as my early recovery.

At home, when I met people at recovery meetings I initially refrained from giving them my phone number, in part due to my husband's discomfort about any of my new friends. I knew that he was generally uncomfortable with telling people that I was an addict. Of course, as I mentioned earlier, I had my own fears about people knowing I was a doctor in recovery. My husband also wanted us to attend a St. Patrick's Day party together, just a week after I had stopped drinking. When I told him that I couldn't go because there were would be drinking there, and I was too fragile to be around alcohol, he got angry about that too.

Day by day, I began to more clearly see that what I wanted and needed in my marriage as a person seeking recovery was not something I was able to receive. I wanted my husband's full support for doing what I had to do to stick with recovery, without fear of what others might think. More than that, I yearned for empathy and support for the physical and emotional challenges during this time when it seemed as if life had been turned upside down. He simply was not able to deliver that. And as I cleared out my brain from the drugs, I could see that he probably had never had been able to do that. In fact, we may have chosen each other in part because we were both fearful of emotional intimacy and wanted to remain somewhat distant and isolated even in the context of a marriage. I have come to understand that many relationships, marriages, parent-child and other, are quite distant. This is not to say that love is any less, but genuine closeness goes missing more that I had realized. Some reading this, especially analytically oriented psychiatrists and therapists may say, yes, but over-involvement, too much closeness, can be intrusive. I am not suggesting absence of boundaries, but the acceptance of "self" enough to share emotionally and spiritually, not just physically, with another person. Becoming vulnerable in this way is frightening. Don't let your fear paralyze you! Keep working on allowing yourself to be emotionally available to loved ones. While not possible to avoid hurt in close relationships, I guarantee you that the joy is worth the fear and pain.

When I was so frequently mind altered I didn't require empathy and support, but things were different now. And, of course, there was the matter of my ex-husband's continued use of alcohol...

We were growing further apart, mostly because I had changed the rules. We were no longer drinking buddies. I was becoming emotionally present, and could not avoid what was in front of me. I invited him to join me at meetings. "We can change together," I implored, to which he replied, "But Dawn, we have it all: work we love, two great kids, a nice home." He did not understand that what was missing was emotional intimacy. We tried marriage counseling. I remember the day the therapist called attention to evidence of one of my behaviors. I was wearing two watches at the time because I knew that one watch was almost dead. Okay, I was still caught in some crazy thinking! Our therapist astutely pointed this out. "You really keep things around until there's no hope, don't you?" she said.

Bingo! I already had pretty much concluded that to remain clean I would ultimately have to leave my marriage. But then I would ask myself, "What are my options? My kids are 7 and 4. It's not a good time to leave. Then, if I dedicate the next 10 years to this marriage and children, they'll be 17 and 14. That's still not a good time. Well, how about 10 more years? Is that a good time?" By then I would have invested 20 more years in an empty marriage. I know couples who choose to do this, even living in separate bedrooms, with no physical or emotional intimacy for years, or even decades. I didn't want that! On the other hand, I also remembered that advice from recovery programs to steer clear of other major life changes for the first year. This was a really tough decision. Still, the choice I had to make was clear. Concluding that there was no good time to do what I knew I had to do for my own emotional and spiritual growth and health, I decided to separate. Most importantly, I had to protect my sobriety. I hung on to the idea that he would see, he would miss me, he would find his own recovery, whatever that meant, and then we could be together again. We could grow together and make up for having grown so apart. That didn't happen, and in my case, leaving, as painful as it was, turned out to be a very positive choice. My recovery became more deeply rooted and eventually, after four years of hard work on my personal growth, I met and married a man who understood recovery and, like me, was seeking a better way to be in a relationship.

I can't tell you what will be right for you if you find yourself in a marriage that does not support your recovery. Perhaps you held on during Phase I Recovery as you focused most of your energy on staying clean and getting healthier, and you're just now ready to take a more serious look at the potential for salvaging your marriage. But whatever you do, I can tell you that it will help to make sure that you're seeing things clearly, that you have spoken up to your spouse about what you need, that you have tried marriage counseling, that you believe in your heart that the choice you are making is the one that you need to make. I know many couples whose marriage has survived and thrived through the recovery of one or both partners. Watching couples celebrate forty, fifty, even sixty years together, half of those in recovery, speaks to the dedication and willingness to work on personal growth as much as it does to deep love and respect for each other. I have been privileged to see this and am thankful for those who serve as my role models for healthy relationships.

And, as with everything else that happens in your recovery, it's critical that you seek out support for what you are going through today and dramatic changes that you may opt to make tomorrow. Others will remind you that while tough choices like these may rock your boat, they also may ultimately enhance your prospects for a Phase II Recovery that truly does allow you to become the person you're meant to be.

When I looked at the roots of my parents' relationship, I could clearly identify some of the wrong moves and warning signs left unnoticed or unaddressed.

Lesson #50
STEER CLEAR OF DESTRUCTIVE MODELS

I've worked with many single or divorced addicts who recognized their paucity of positive role models for healthy relationships, and sincerely wanted to practice a new way in their next relationship. But then they met someone and they rushed toward intimacy and, after a brief honeymoon phase when they were convinced they were doing it right, something went wrong. When they looked around, they saw that they had somehow repeated many of the same mistakes that had undermined either their previous relationships or, as is so often the case, the relationships of those who had influenced them—or both. In other words, they were following the wrong models again. Doing the same things and expecting different results is one definition of insanity!

When I looked at the roots of my parents' relationship, I could clearly identify some of the wrong moves and warning signs left unnoticed or unaddressed. This is what I learned from my mother about how she and my father came together: My mother had left rural North Carolina to come north to the big city of Baltimore to find her fame as a newspaper reporter. In 1939 she met Fred, a fun guy who played the banjo in a band and seemed to know everyone. They spent many enjoyable evenings dancing and dining. He introduced her to Maryland soft shell crabs as well as a slew of fascinating people.

Soon she moved to Washington, DC to follow her dream job with the Washington Post, and even seemed to be in line for a post as foreign correspondent in Europe, where World War II had begun. But Fred asked her to marry him, and looking back she recognized that he had an ulterior motive. Single men were the first to be drafted. "If you don't marry me, I'm not responsible for what happens," he laughed regarding the draft. But maybe it was no joke—maybe he was threatening to marry someone else, just to change his draft status. Mom succumbed to the pressure from him to do what he wanted, forsaking her career as a top-level journalist. She had lost herself, and the downward spiral of her life in relationship with my father had begun.

In my own first marriage, I had found a drinking buddy and someone who understood and accepted my work schedule. Beyond that, we had little in common. After my divorce, I was determined to do future relationships differently. When I met Erik, we both acknowledged that we wanted more than an ordinary relationship. He said he did not want a boring relationship and furthermore wanted to heed his father's caution to marry someone who was kind. While not perfect, we have both worked hard to be kind to each other and everyone else and have definitely not been bored. From the outset, we were consciously aligned in wanting the very best for each other and living in a mutually supportive and respectful union.

So wherever you may be in your own relationship cycle, remind yourself this: You can do it differently now, with the same person or with someone new. Spend time identifying what went wrong in your own failed relationships and those you have observed. Underline the parts that most tell the story, and jot down notes on what would make it different. Look at yourself and what you have learned in the Twelve Steps. Keep your eyes wide open when any potential relationship beckons, and be brutally honest about how it does, or does not fit the trail you are blazing in Phase II Recovery.

Lesson #51
DON'T SETTLE FOR ORDINARY

"I don't want an ordinary marriage." Those were the words Erik spoke to me before we were married. Truth be told, I didn't really have a clear idea what he meant back then. But, I figured, if ordinary meant "blah" at best, and divorced at worst, I might as well sign on to something better. And since we wed in 1989, our marriage has not been ordinary at all—it has been extraordinary!

As two partners both in recovery, we took heed of the importance of finding the ingredients of a healthy relationship and we reached for them every day and night. We've worked especially hard at setting limits and boundaries and not blaming the other for what we do or how we feel. Erik has been consistently supportive of my work as an MD, initially in Family Practice and now as an Addictionist as well, never complaining when the needs of my patients sometimes took precedence over a chance to be together. He's been an integral part of my medical missions overseas, making for some extraordinary shared experiences.

If you are single and open to the possibility of finding a new partner in Phase II Recovery, I urge you not to settle for ordinary either. Get clear on the mistakes you want to avoid repeating, recognizing that the work to make those changes is yours to do and doesn't end because you think you have found the "right" person. Spend time with any prospective partner discussing your relationship history and your ideas of what matters most to you in any new attempt. Hold firm to the need to only commit to relationships that will support your recovery and be bold enough to aim high!

Of course, the final frontier of relationships also encompasses all those ongoing relationships with family members and others who remain part of your life. You may not be able to lift them all to the extraordinary level, but you can certainly do your part to try to make them better and different from what they had been. The basic recovery work of making amends (remember, this word means to change) is a terrific start. Just as important is to become aware of how you are dealing with the other person in the here and now, and what you can do to break any negative cycles to which each of you contributed.

Remember that list of a few of the ingredients of healthy relationships at the start of this section? Reread it. Before beginning a relationship, take time out—as much time as needed, maybe even a whole year—and develop those ingredients with yourself. Become honest, respectful, and caring of yourself. Only then can you give away the very qualities you want in a relationship with another person. Remember, we are attracted to our emotional equals. As you grow and develop in these healthy relationship qualities, you will attract and be attracted to other healthy people, those who can give back what you give to them.

In an earlier lesson I shared the story of Ed, a patient I was counseling in the aftermath of a disappointing reunion with his brother who lived far away. Ed came away from their visit feeling sad about not finding the closeness he yearned for with his brother, but he was tempted to blame his brother for it. I reminded him that the principle of not blaming the other is a cornerstone of healthy relationships and that Ed needed to see how he could behave differently to enhance the chances of getting what he wanted.

You have that same opportunity today in your relationships with your family, friends, co-workers and others. Through your dedicated efforts in recovery, you are learning the tools of how to be a better person and how to create more positive relationships. You can make the first move that can open the door to change. I remember about ten years ago when I was feeling disappointed in some of the dynamics of my relationship with my brother Fred. In my commitment to my recovery, I concluded that it was not acceptable for me to have the relationship continue to follow the direction in which it was headed. Gathering my courage, I requested that Fred join me in attending a relationship workshop, and I'm so grateful that he agreed.

After we worked through some differences and moved to a new ground, I thought about the many families that suffer cut-offs in their relationships and don't do anything about it. The truth is, we in recovery are especially well equipped for choosing a different way. On this final frontier, we can truly be pioneers!

Many addicts in Phase II Recovery embark on new and more fulfilling careers.

Section 10: Expanding Your Horizons

Lesson #52

IF THERE WAS EVER ANYTHING YOU HAD DREAMED OF DOING, DO IT NOW

When I first dreamed of becoming a doctor at age 12, I had a vivid image of what that would look like. I was going to be a medical missionary, practicing medicine in some Third World country, probably in Africa, where people had been deprived of real medical care for all or most of their lives. I clung to this image all the way to med school, though it then dissolved into "life on automatic." I did an internship and residency, got married, established a family practice, had two children…doing what was familiar and in front of me. For nearly two decades, I seldom thought of that ancient dream. It was there, though, waiting to be resuscitated.

Then one day, well into my recovery, I was flipping through a medical journal during my lunch break at my family medicine office in suburban Denver when I came across this ad: "Physician Wanted for short-term Medical Mission to Honduras". With sweaty palms and pounding heart, I instantly wondered: could I really consider picking up my dream and head off to another country, in a developing part of the world, as a volunteer doctor? It didn't take me long to decide. When I got home that day I announced to Erik, "I'm going to Honduras! Want to come?" I followed up that stint in Honduras with medical missions in Ecuador, Bolivia, Viet Nam, Brazil, and Indonesia. Each mission has been short term, never taking me away from my own medical practice or family for more than a few weeks.

While I never could have reached out to reclaim that childhood dream while riding the roller coaster of Phase I Recovery, I had the capacity to follow the dream and the adventure, to step out of my secure and familiar world and jump at the chance in Phase II Recovery.

That's how different life can be in Phase II: things that would have been impossible in active addiction or early recovery suddenly seem within reach and even fully attainable. As I write this, I recently returned from the mission closest to my original dream: the African country of Kenya. Each mission taught me more, and gave me more, than I possibly could give those I treated. I was especially grateful in these foreign lands to meet and share with others on the road to recovery. More than once, we held candlelight recovery meetings on the kitchen table of whatever dwelling we found ourselves in. After each mission I wonder if it will be my last, a question that lingers only until the next one is in front of me.

The recovery community does a wonderful job of encouraging addicts in recovery to identify former dreams and go after them. This is a perfect complement to any Phase II Recovery. I remember my friend Jeanne talking about how hard it was to acknowledge that she was a drug addict at age 23. She had never been aware of any dreams or ambitions, just focusing for many years on getting high, escaping reality, and certainly not attending school. Then, working hard throughout her early recovery, she was able to move to her own Phase II rapidly. With prompting from others in her recovery circle, pushing her with questions about what she wanted to do with her life, she realized she wanted to be a teacher. She began school and persisted in getting several degrees, all the while maintaining a healthy recovery. She has now been a well-respected Special Education teacher for more than 25 years, touching the lives of students, parents, and fellow teachers with far-reaching, positive influence. As with many of us, part of who Jeanne is comes from the valuable lessons of recovery and the wisdom gained from sharing the journey with others. She remains active in recovery circles, attending meetings and sponsoring people.

Many addicts in Phase II Recovery embark on new and more fulfilling careers. In Phase I Recovery, we looked at how getting clean enables addicts to be better at work they do every day. In Phase II Recovery, we can see how having the strength and energy to broaden our horizons can open the door to exciting new kinds of work.

Your former dream does not have to be focused on helping the needy, and it may not be career related at all. It can be anything that energizes you and helps you celebrate where you are, and where you're

216

going in your own version of Phase II Recovery. One friend told me that for years he had a dream of owning and riding a Honda Goldwing touring motorcycle. Friends urged him to go for it, and it wasn't long before he was coming around our house and offering to take my two very excited daughters out for a ride.

When you ask yourself if there is anything you had dreamed of doing but didn't because your addiction got in the way, or that you held off during the fragile period of Phase I Recovery, you may know the answer right away. If you don't, be patient. Ask a second time, and a third. The right response will emerge. And then it's up to you to find a way to make it happen!

With all the medical and technological advances of the last few decades, we really are living longer and healthier.

Lesson #53
NO MATTER YOUR AGE, YOU CAN CONTINUE TO REFINE YOUR RECOVERY

"This is as good as it gets." That's the slogan, usually unspoken, by which addicts who don't strive to move beyond Phase I Recovery are living. They're clean. They're keeping out of trouble. They're holding onto a job, staying in school, getting connected with family again. They're going to meetings and saying and doing the right things. They're not fighting major despair or depression.

All these states of being are completely worth honoring, even celebrating. But the key to living an uplifting Phase II Recovery is to believe that in your life without drugs you have an opportunity for something more. I can't tell you what that something more will look like. Only you will know that, and you will discover it by continuing to explore, and to trust in yourself, or in God, as you know Him, or just in life. And that opportunity is there whether you happen to be just out of your teens, in early adulthood, in mid-life, or well into the retirement zone. You are never too young or too old to claim recovery and you are never too young or too old to refine your recovery.

Many older recovering addicts scoff at this notion. They start working the steps and they get to the parts about taking moral inventory and the personal, emotional, and spiritual growth that appears obtainable, and they shake their heads. "I'm 75 years old," they may say. "These habits are entrenched for decades. I can stop using alcohol and drugs but as for the rest of my ways of thinking and behaving, it's too late to change." And I think, how sad. My mother was in her 70s when she died, still an active alcoholic. What I would have given to see her enjoy even one year of living clean, and the changes that recovery may have ushered in. Conversely, my father's youngest sister sobered up at age 72. She had six fabulous years of healthy recovery before her death of natural causes.

I'm going to make my case to you for taking the full ride of recovery, no matter your age, not just on an emotional appeal but on factual evidence. Consider the changes in life expectancy rates. As we all can see every day, we seem to be living longer. The latest statistics I saw indicated the average life expectancy in the U.S. is now 78 years old and projected to reach the 80s in the near future. That's up roughly 10 years since the 1980s, and back in 1900, life expectancy was only in the 40s. We all have known family members, friends, or members of our social or religious communities who have lived well into their 90s—or longer. With all the medical and technological advances of the last few decades, we really are living longer and healthier.

Think about what that means. If you enter recovery at age 50, you could easily be looking at the opportunities of 30 or more years in recovery! And even if you're in your 60s and 70s when you get clean, there's a pretty good chance you may have a solid one or two decades to enjoy living without drugs, especially now that you've taken such a sharp turn toward physical health and well-being. You've got time to become more and more of that person you were meant to be. Maybe you won't be turning somersaults or cranking up rock music on your iPad (but maybe you will!), but you sure can take on many new realms of emotional and spiritual growth and begin important undertakings that you had long since crossed off your list during your years of addiction. You do have time. And you will deeply appreciate the major changes that for decades remained unattainable.

Freedom from age limits for a rich Phase II Recovery also applies to those at the younger end of the spectrum. Many addicts in their 20s or 30s regret how their childhood or adolescent ambitions blew up because of their addiction. They fear that since they didn't follow the "regular" routine of college education and professional training, they've missed the boat for good. Not true. So you missed out on five or ten years. You've got lots of time to catch up, and your motivation and commitment are likely to be much higher now than if you had pursued a career goal right out of high school. Plus, the truth is that you had to go through whatever you suffered to get here.

So no matter how young or old you may be, or even how many years you have been in recovery before you sense that you are shifting to Phase II, you've got time. If you live by recovery thinking, recovery speaking, and recovery living every day, you can't help but continue to change and grow. It is the gift you have given yourself, and the gift that has been given to you. As we cover the final round of lessons, do not forget that.

Only you know in your heart and soul which route to God is right for you, or which to try.

Lesson #54
KEEP FOLLOWING YOUR OWN SPIRITUAL PATH

It's time to come back to the "G" word. We need to take a little more time exploring God and spirituality because, just as having a relationship with some concept of God is critical to practicing the Twelve Steps and solidifying Phase I Recovery, it is just as critical to have a spiritual foundation when you seek to expand your growth and fully experience the possibilities of a vibrant Phase II Recovery.

While I was writing an article on spirituality for my former newspaper column, now posted on my website (www.docdawn.com), I decided to look up the definition of "spirit." One dictionary provided 14 different definitions. I was reminded that the base word comes from the Latin word spirare, which means, "to breathe." Well, we all do that, every minute of our lives. Maybe that's an indication of just how basic spirituality is to us. We need it, can't live without it, and it's totally natural. There are countless routes to spiritual health that an addict in Phase II Recovery may pursue for the first time, or engage in more earnestly than during Phase I or any other period of life. There are many principles to apply in seeking to live a more spiritual life. Some that I have found especially important for my patients and myself include: don't judge, don't compare, and don't have a need to know why.

When I consider a concept such as "don't judge," I immediately relate it to questions about God, questions many addicts benefit from asking and pondering. As human beings, we are not in charge of the Universe. Try saying this, "There is a God and it's not me." As we discussed earlier, if you find the word "God" objectionable, you can simply substitute "Force of the Universe" or "Nature" or something else you can accept. The point is that the sun rises and sets and you are not in charge of it. The only things we are in charge of are our own behavior, our thoughts, and sometimes our feelings. So if we judge another person or situation, we are trying to play God. If we can let God do the judging, we find we can be more open-minded. We can see what people do simply as behavior, something they are just doing, not doing to us. This perspective not only allows others to be more real to us, it also allows us to be the best person we can be. By not judging, we can treat all people equally and fairly, stop regarding ourselves as victims, and let God be in charge.

Those other key concepts also easily relate to God. When we don't compare ourselves to others, we can see ourselves and everyone else as God's kids, playing down here in His sandbox, chopping wood and hauling water, doing the best we can with what we have to work with. When we don't need to know why, we stop regretting yesterday and worrying about tomorrow. The idea that God has a plan and that we don't get to know what it is until it happens is liberating, leading us ever closer to being the best we can be in the here and now, and opening the door to more joy and peace. And when we choose to live by trust we are making the statement that God will give us the spiritual strength and capacity to get through whatever new challenge confronts us.

Only you know in your heart and soul which route to God is right for you, or which to try. I shared with you in our exploration of Phase I Recovery how I struggled with the "G" word early in my recovery before I slowly formed a relationship with God that continues to grow and expand. Today I can say that I am not only spiritual but also religious. I am a Christian, though I still struggle with some of the beliefs and practices of many Christian faiths, individuals, and specific churches. As various ministers and church leaders can attest, I ask a lot of questions! One answer that has been crystal clear, however, is that my deeper relationship with God has elevated everything in my life. It's a cornerstone of my Phase II Recovery. It may be that for you too.

Lesson #55
OPEN THE GATE OF FORGIVENESS

I'd like to share with you two stories that illustrate the power of forgiveness in Phase II Recovery. Here's the first story:

Several years ago, my husband Erik and I bought some land in Colorado. There was an old homestead and several outbuildings on the land, and our contract stated that all the farm and ranch equipment would become ours at the purchase. The owner of the land had died, leaving it to his wife and family. Though the sale to us did go through, one daughter, Liz, opposed it. We learned that she had been the "black sheep" of the family and that she had an infant buried on the land. Interestingly, she also happened to be an alcoholic.

Before we physically claimed our new property, Liz expressed her anger and sadness over the sale by stealing a tractor, cook stove, pile driver, and other items that were part of the purchase, and selling them to nearby ranchers. During the ensuing legal action, we heard that Liz had gone into treatment for her alcoholism. We prayed that she would make it into recovery and embrace a clean, happy, responsible life. A year later the judge awarded us a portion of what we asked for, which was perfectly acceptable to us. Immediately following the court action, literally minutes later, she and I both went to the ladies room I met Liz for the first time.

"Are you okay?" I asked.

"Yes," she said, "and I hope what I did has not taken away your pleasure in owning the land."

"Not at all," I said. "Are you sober?"

Liz proudly pulled from her pocket her one-year sobriety coin, and after whooping my congratulations and hugging her, I pulled out my 20-year sobriety coin. We have gone on to become friends and, recognizing her enduring connection to the land, we gave her permission to visit whenever she wants to and lets us know in advance. We even gave her the gate code to get in. I completely forgave her…how could I not? It's nice to be forgiven, and so much nicer to forgive! This has become one experience of new gates literally opening through the act of forgiveness.

Now, for the second story. In the section of lessons on re-solving your past, I shared with you how I had come to be able to release my old pain, anger, and blame toward my parents and forgive them, seeing them as two people who had many good qualities and did the best they could. I feel so blessed that this act of forgiveness happened while they were still alive.…

While Mom never did choose recovery, I chose to change my relationship with her. My commitment was to accept her as she was—nothing better, nothing worse. And soon after my divorce and moving into a new home with my two daughters, I had a chance to practice this kind of forgiveness in action. Her health was declining, and she was still drinking while we exchanged visits in Colorado and Baltimore. I stopped being critical and dropped my expectations of her. I can't tell you how good that felt. When we visited her and she struggled to even get a can of soup on the table, instead of judging and grumbling I said, "Man this is really good soup!" The last time she visited us, just days before her cancer diagnosis, I took coffee to her in the basement guestroom the first morning she was with us. Amid tears she said, "No one ever did this for me." When her colon cancer took hold and we knew the end was coming swiftly, I would fly back East every other Thursday night and stay with her until flying back home in time for my Sunday night NA meeting. In the final days, remembering how she had been baptized by her minister father in a river in North Carolina, my brother and I brought her to a motel where she could swim in the pool up until her very last days alive. When she died, I was at peace, a peace made possible by forgiveness.

My father was already in a fragile state when Mom died. He had actually stopped drinking during his final year, but the damage to his body had been done. When the news of his death reached me, nine months after Mom's, I was in Austin, Texas, where I was competing in

226

a masters swimming event. "I've got to get to the airport right away!" I shouted. It was late at night and I did not even call to try to buy a ticket. With the help of a kind soul at the swim meet, I raced to the airport, ran down the corridor (pre-airport security of course), and reached the gate just as the pilot was about to board and the gate attendant was about to complete the boarding. Tears streaming down my face, and a credit card dangling from my hands, I stammered, "My Dad just died. I've got to get to Baltimore—right away!" Not only did they take me on the flight, they put me in First Class. I don't think they ever charged me for the ticket. Without their kindness, I never would have gotten home that night. Without my forgiveness, I never would have found myself experiencing such a moving and memorable moment.

I offer these stories to you as a reminder. We don't forgive just to be a better person in our recovery. We forgive because the act of forgiveness opens the gate to a better life.

And when we respond with kindness, caring, and generosity, we experience and can appreciate the profound change in our way of being.

Lesson #56
DO WELL BY OTHERS
BECAUSE OF WHO YOU ARE

Okay, I've shared many stories about my own life in recovery to help you learn from my particular experience. It's about time I tell a story about my wonderful husband Erik. Last winter Erik pulled a neighbor woman in a large car out of a ditch. She had skidded off our snow-packed road here in snowy northwestern Colorado, hitting a patch of ice beneath the fairly benign looking layer of snow. We live in a rural area where neighbors are few and spread out over many acres and miles, and when she called for help, Erik was quick to respond.

Sounds like a basic friendly deed for a neighbor, right? A little background here: on several previous occasions I had asked this same neighbor to do a minor favor for me; each time she said no. We continued to be cordial, but I stopped pursuing a friendship with her. One of my requests that she denied was to keep her dogs off my property, as they were not only chasing and scaring away the wildlife but had actually killed several fawns! I found my own way—a peaceful way— to deal with that, asking the Division of Wildlife to intervene. It turns out that it is not only illegal to allow dogs to harass or kill wildlife, but illegal to allow them to run free.

On that cold and snowy morning that she called, however, Erik never hesitated. He put on warm clothes, got in his truck, drove the two miles to the location she described, and did the hard work of getting her car free, while she watched him from her toasty perch inside her car talking on her cell phone. On top of that, he nearly got his own truck stuck in the process. When Erik got home more than two hours later—wet, dirty, and tired—I asked him how difficult it was to summon the compassion and willingness to help this same woman who had been unwilling to help us. "I did it because of who I am," he explained, "not because of who she is."

Leave it to my husband to illustrate through such a simple gesture the power of shifting our perspective as an addict traveling well down the road of recovery. Instead of our former ways of being quick to judge, blame, and criticize others for their behavior, we can not only accept them as people but also reach out to them as human beings with needs of their own—needs that we will often find ourselves in position to meet. And when we respond with kindness, caring, and generosity, we experience and can appreciate the profound change in our way of being. When we were drinking and drugging, the world was all about us and our needs. Our selfishness and self-absorption dictated our response to the people and situations around us. Now we have the ability to relate to the world around us from an entirely new and different foundation: loving kindness, the instinct to act according to what we know is right.

Thanks for helping us see this lesson, Erik!

Section 11: Sharing the Gift

Lesson #57
IF YOU HAVE AN INSTINCT TO HELP HEAL OTHERS, HONOR IT

When you're in Phase II Recovery, it often seems as if life is all about one new choice after another. Many of those new choices catch us by surprise because during our days of drugging, we could never have envisioned holding them in our hands. Take, for example, a dynamic I see often in my community of recovering addicts. The very addicts who spent years convinced that they could never heal themselves, or who used denial to bury a belief that no one was capable or willing to do anything to help them, now feel a compelling urge to try to help others to recover and heal.

Have you noticed this happening to you? Have you explored how you might act on that urge? If not, and you are strong and confident enough in your own recovery, this may be the time to look around and see how and where you might put those instincts to heal to use. You might find that love multiplies as we give it away. More importantly, we have to give it away to keep it, in life and in recovery.

Recovery circles encourage us to help others get clean and stay clean as a natural part of the supportive environments that emerge through Twelve Step meetings. Offering encouragement and the hope drawn from our own experiences to those struggling to break free from addiction feels gratifying. Who would have thought we could help make a positive difference in someone else's life? The opportunity to help may extend beyond attending recovery meetings. Maybe you'll decide to go back to school to gain the training and credentials to join a healing or helping profession. Maybe you'll find yourself offering inspiration through lectures and talks to diverse groups. Or perhaps you'll just find opportunities to informally call upon who you are and what you have lived through to be of service to those around you. By being visible in the recovery community, you may be asked to sponsor others. This is a terrific way to be of service as well as to reinforce your own recovery. You can assist addicts wanting recovery, as well as others, who will be astounded to hear about how your life used to look and how it has changed.

I was already working as a healthcare professional when I entered recovery, but the transition in becoming an MD Addictionist was certainly not something I could have foreseen. I didn't even plan to make the change—it just happened as more and more people would show up in my office because they knew what I had gone through: the pain of growing up in an alcoholic family, my own years of active addiction, my suicide attempts, and most important, my ongoing recovery. I embraced the choice to shift my professional emphasis in this new direction, and I'm continually touched by all the new roles I have ·the opportunity to play. It's a privilege just to witness and somehow be helpful to addicts doing the hard work to transform their lives.

Sometimes a special moment comes along that just makes me smile. I mentioned earlier my role in helping local recovering sex addicts' to form their own support group. One day one of the group's members called me and, temporarily forgetting the number he had dialed and thinking he had reached his wife, said "Hi, Honey." After we both laughed, he said, "At least you know I am calling my wife, not some random woman." I happened to tell Erik about it and not long thereafter he and Erik were at an AA meeting together. "So," Erik said in mock seriousness, "I heard you call my wife Honey, huh?" Both men laughed at the honest mistake.

Erik has used his own capacity to help others, and sometimes our work converges in spontaneous ways. When my daughter Brie was in high school, I was often called upon as a resource for school counselors. I spoke at other schools in our district, but when I was invited to speak at her school I asked her permission. Brie enthusiastically encouraged me to come, knowing I would be discussing my own addiction and recovery. She even made a courageous decision to share her own experiences growing up in an alcoholic household where mother and stepfather were in recovery. I was so proud of her, seeing her demonstrate openness in front of teachers and classmates, and realizing she had no need to keep secrets. Uplifted by the idea that in that hour we might make a difference in some teenager's life, perhaps steering them away from the destructive path of addiction, or providing hope for enduring any painful condition at home, I wasn't prepared for the carry-over effect.

Whether from my talks or simply meeting us when they visited our home, teenagers began spending more time with Erik and me. The boys were especially fond of Erik. Several of them have since told us, now that they are adults in their thirties, that our home was a safe and comfortable place for them. Some have come to us specifically to let us know that we helped them survive their teen years and contributed to their becoming responsible, healthy adults. A few even stayed with us for several weeks, retreating from their dysfunctional homes, but most just came over to eat cookies and talk, whether Brie and Kara were home or not! We often had a table full of teens for an evening meal of pizza, pasta or some other favorite. Erik and I were approachable, non-judgmental, and emotionally available for discussions about anything. As we cleaned up after one typical evening with assorted high schoolers, I shook my head and said, "Who would have ever thought that the home of two former druggies would be the place teenagers would love to hang out, where they couldn't drink or even smoke?"

It's another way that we addicts who are secure in our recovery, and who feel the urge to help others heal, can rewrite our old scripts. Instead of being the life of the party where we beckon others to join us in drinking and drugging, we can become the oasis where those in need can openly share their struggles and drink in nurturing and encouragement. Sound like a choice you'd like to look into a bit further?

Consider displaying the recovery bumper stickers, wearing the t-shirts and using the sayings.

Lesson #58
CONTRIBUTE TO THE CAUSE
OF RECOVERY

Of all the ways that you might consider lending your help and support to others in need, you certainly don't want to forget those places and people that you may know best: addiction treatment centers or anywhere else where addicts are the focus of healing efforts. The people there are those you know and understand, with experiences similar to yours. You can grasp not only their pain but also their possibilities. You know all their tricks too. If there is work you can do there, if not in a professional counseling capacity then in an administrative or volunteer role, you may find the experience especially rewarding. More important, you will know that you are having a direct effect on human lives and contributing to the cause of recovery.

If working in and around the field of addiction is not appealing to you, finding ways to be the best human being you can be, wherever you work and play, may put opportunities you don't expect in front of you. People in need are everywhere. Addicts, alcoholics, and those struggling to survive in a family or relationship with an addict are around every corner. You will find that you can help, simply by sharing your own experience with recovery. Of course, you can always be helpful to the rest of the human beings out there, too — the "normies". Guaranteed.

A 2005 estimate provided by the National Institute on Alcohol Abuse and Addiction indicated that just over one-third of all alcoholics are in recovery. That doesn't even take into account those still using other mind-altering substances, where estimates of those finding recovery tend to run lower. As I mentioned earlier, such estimates are really just guesses. We don't know how many men and women may be suffering and in need of recovery today. We really only know two things: 1) The need is great; 2) We who have traveled the road to recovery are usually the most qualified and the most motivated to help. So keep going to meetings, not only for yourself but for those newcomers who may look at you as one of their primary sources of hope and inspiration. You may be the one—you may have the story to tell—that pulls them into the net of recovery. Show up. Be real. Be yourself. Consider displaying the recovery bumper stickers, wearing the t-shirts and using the sayings. Maintain your commitment and your enthusiasm for the courageous community that has served you. You never know when and how you may be making a difference.

Lesson #59
SOAK UP THE
MAGICAL MOMENTS

As addicts committed to long-term recovery and becoming the person we were meant to be, we appreciate those special moments that mark the trail of Phase II Recovery. They serve as another sign of the 180 degree turn of our life's portfolio. Years ago the moments that stuck with us most likely were marked by suffering or shame. Today the moments that stand out are marked by joy and gratitude. And more.

During our lessons on Phase I Recovery, I shared with you how I began competitive swimming because I could not sleep well and was always up before 5 a.m. The adult (masters) team practiced just blocks from my home. As a result, my endorphins (brain chemicals that fight depression and drug hunger) kicked in every day, I stopped smoking cigarettes, and my physical health improved. Some of the women on my swim team would talk about another fitness endeavor they had chosen to pursue: triathlons. Could I do that too? I mean, I already had the swimming part going, and I knew how to ride a bike. But the third component of triathlons is running. Uh, maybe not. So I looked for competitive events that only entailed swimming and biking, but when I didn't find any around, I said, "Okay, another challenge." In my mid-40s at the time, I established a goal to complete a triathlon by age 50.

So I decided to dig in my heels and figure out how to become a runner. The first time I tried, I couldn't even make it around the quarter-mile track. Heidi, a neighbor and experienced runner was willing to show me the ropes. Slowly I was working my way up to entering 5K races, just 3.1 mile runs, where I amazed myself by reaching the finish line in one piece! That was encouraging, especially since that was the distance of the running part of the sprint distance triathlons. Yes, I met my goal of completing a triathlon—actually, many triathlons—by age 50.

The next step up for me in triathlon competition was to the olympic distance, double the distance of the sprint in each of the three sports, swimming, cycling and running. I actually found that I was doing better with the longer distances, and when my friend Roger directed me to check out the times for women in my age group who competed nationally, I set a new goal: qualifying for the U.S. National team. At first I fell just short due to a mechanical problem with my bike. Ugh. Resigned to not making the team, I was stunned and overjoyed when I got a call—I was invited to join the US Triathlon Amateur Team at the 2000 world championships in Perth, Australia! Even as an amateur, an older one at that, I enjoyed some magical moments there, feeling like a real athlete, and that spurred me on to reach for the top rung of triathlon competition: the Ironman Triathlon. Undaunted by one injury that caused a setback along the way, in 2003 I entered Ironman Brazil.

So there I was in the resort town of Florianopolis, Brazil, the country where my husband Erik grew up, rising up for a true test of my endurance and strength: a 2.4 mile ocean swim, a 112-mile bike ride, and a 26.2 mile run. I was tanned, toned, buffed, and ready.

Usually, I found the swimming segment the most manageable part, but the Brazilian ocean waters that day were cold and rough, with unrelenting waves. I was fighting and struggling, my heart racing. This was no way to engage in something I had aimed for so long.

And then an image flashed before me: I was five years old in the ocean waters of Maryland with my father, still sober under the early morning sun. He had escorted me past the breakers to a sandbar, and as he would back up he would beckon me. "Swim to me, Dawnsie," he said. "Swim to me." I'd swim toward him and he'd playfully back up a little, and then a little more, never allowing me to get scared or frustrated. He made it all just a wonderful game. We kept on playing in those waves, going up and over, floating, then going under and diving through them.

That's all it took. I made a choice to change my thinking, to alter my relationship with the rough, cold waves of Brazil. In an instant, I was transformed to a little girl playing in the waves. Up and over. An easy, natural rhythm. Swim to me, Dawnsie. When I finished the swimming leg, I was beaming. My momentum swept on to the biking and marathon run, and I went on to a second place finish in my age group. My coach asked me if I was disappointed at not finishing first. Was she kidding? I had just been gifted by a combination of forces and events that gave me chills at knowing how far I had come in my physical, emotional, and spiritual growth. I was soaking up one of the truly magical moments of my entire life.

Where and when have you been touched by magical moments in Phase II Recovery? When they come, make sure you stop and savor them. Share them with others close to you. And drop me a line. I'd love to hear about them too.

For whatever reason, I was able to accept the path offered to me. I'm so grateful to have a relationship with God today and that I have been given the gift of ongoing recovery.

Lesson #60
CELEBRATE YOUR SUCCESS

As the years go by in your recovery, and you notice that your new life without alcohol and drugs has gone on as long or longer than your life while using, you will be blessed with many opportunities to celebrate your success. They may come in the form of milestones related to anniversary dates of being clean and sober. They may come via a new achievement you have worked hard for and recognize you never could have reached without recovery. They may come on a birthday or some other event where friends and loved ones are expressing their love for you and how much they value having you in their lives. When such opportunities come, embrace them. You also may choose to use the moment to reflect back on how far you've come and to express your gratitude for this gift of recovery.

I've been fortunate enough to enjoy many of these opportunities in Phase II Recovery. I'll share one recent experience. I was on another medical mission, this one to Kenya. The group organizing the mission asked the seven of us on the staff to prepare worship services in rotation. When I was assigned the service for March 10, I politely asked if it could be changed to March 9—my 27th anniversary of recovery. After being granted my request, I prepared for the day. Seeing a lot of avocados in the kitchen, I asked if I could use some of them to make a special avocado dessert — avocados mashed with milk and sugar in a pudding. Sounds strange, but this is a great recipe from Erik's mother from the years his family lived in Brazil, where avocados are the size of footballs. As usual, I had brought homemade cookies in my luggage, so I could share them as well. With the green light on that front, I focused on my presentation. I read a passage from The Serenity Bible, a companion to Twelve Step recovery. Then I told everyone about that dream I had at 12 years old to become a doctor and to be a missionary in Africa.

"Well, it's 50 years later and I'm finally here!" I proclaimed with a few tears of joy. "My dream is happening right now, at the right place, with the right people, and at the right time. I don't feel any regret, no lament of 'Oh God, I should have been here 40 years ago.' All I feel is joy, and gratitude. I wouldn't be here at all now, and I wouldn't be married to Erik, if not for my recovery that began 27 years ago today. Every day is a gift—I know if life were 'fair' I would have died from addiction long ago. Instead, the God that I didn't believe in back then directed me to recovery and, for whatever reason, I was able to accept the path offered to me. I'm so grateful to have a relationship with God today and that I have been given the gift of ongoing recovery."

And then everyone sang "Happy Birthday" and we drove through the game park near our mission site, where I got to see elephants, zebras, baboons, and more on the way to work. Adding to the euphoria, I was also able to be present for mission members who approached me after my talk to confide in me something about addiction and recovery, depression, and other struggles, either in their own lives or that of a loved one. Once again, I was able to be of service, to help others be heard, to have a question answered, to gain some insight, some new kernel of truth that could nudge them further along their own recovery path.

That is the spirit in which I have offered this book to you as well. May it serve to enhance your own Phase I and Phase II Recovery, and may you be blessed with many days and many ways to celebrate your success!

ABOUT THE AUTHOR

 Dawn V. Obrecht, M.D., was graduated from the University Of Maryland School Of Medicine and did an internship in general surgery and residency in emergency medicine. She has been the medical director of a chemical dependency unit and is a professor at the University of Colorado Health Sciences Center. For many years she had a busy family medicine practice. Licensed in several states, she now travels to small, rural communities, filling in for physicians who need time off.

Having been in recovery from drug addiction for over a quarter century, Dr. Obrecht uses her experience with life-threatening illness to identify with and help others to heal and to hear God. DocDawn lives in Steamboat Springs, Colorado, with her husband, Erik Landvik, where she writes and consults in addiction medicine between her travels.

FROM THE EDGE OF THE CLIFF

APPENDIX

Long Definition of Addiction

(American Society of Addiction Medicine, April 2011)

Addiction is a primary, chronic disease of brain reward, motivation, memory and related circuitry. Addiction affects neurotransmission and interactions within reward structures of the brain, including the nucleus accumbens, anterior cingulate cortex, basal forebrain and amygdala, such that motivational hierarchies are altered and addictive behaviors, which may or may not include alcohol and other drug use, supplant healthy, self-care related behaviors. Addiction also affects neurotransmission and interactions between cortical and hippocampal circuits and brain reward structures, such that the memory of previous exposures to rewards (such as food, sex, alcohol and other drugs) leads to a biological and behavioral response to external cues, in turn triggering craving and/or engagement in addictive behaviors.

The neurobiology of addiction encompasses more than the neurochemistry of reward.[1] The frontal cortex of the brain and underlying white matter connections between the frontal cortex and circuits of reward, motivation and memory are fundamental in the manifestations of altered impulse control, altered judgment, and the dysfunctional pursuit of rewards (which is often experienced by the affected person as a desire to "be normal") seen in addiction--despite cumulative adverse consequences experienced from engagement in substance use and other addictive behaviors. The frontal lobes are important in inhibiting impulsivity and in assisting individuals to appropriately delay gratification. When persons with addiction manifest problems in deferring gratification, there is a neurological locus of these problems in the frontal cortex. Frontal lobe morphology, connectivity and functioning are still in the process of maturation during adolescence and young adulthood, and early exposure to substance use is another significant factor in the development of addiction. Many neuroscientists believe that developmental morphology is the basis that makes early-life exposure to substances such an important factor.

247

Genetic factors account for about half of the likelihood that an individual will develop addiction. Environmental factors interact with the person's biology and affect the extent to which genetic factors exert their influence. Resiliencies the individual acquires (through parenting or later life experiences) can affect the extent to which genetic predispositions lead to the behavioral and other manifestations of addiction.

Culture also plays a role in how addiction becomes actualized in persons with biological vulnerabilities to the development of addiction.

Other factors that can contribute to the appearance of addiction, leading to its characteristic bio-psycho-socio-spiritual manifestations, include:

a) The presence of an underlying biological deficit in the function of reward circuits, such that drugs and behaviors which enhance reward function are preferred and sought as reinforcers;

b) The repeated engagement in drug use or other addictive behaviors, causing neuroadaptation in motivational circuitry leading to impaired control over further drug use or engagement in addictive behaviors;

c) Cognitive and affective distortions, which impair perceptions and compromise the ability to deal with feelings, resulting in significant self-deception;

d) Disruption of healthy social supports and problems in interpersonal relationships which impact the development or impact of resiliencies;

e) Exposure to trauma or stressors that overwhelm an individual's coping abilities;

f) Distortion in meaning, purpose and values that guide attitudes, thinking and behavior;

g) Distortions in a person's connection with self, with others and with the transcendent (referred to as God by many, the Higher Power by 12-steps groups, or higher consciousness by others); and

h) The presence of co-occurring psychiatric disorders in persons who engage in substance use or other addictive behaviors.

Addiction is characterized by[2]:

a) **Inability to consistently <u>A</u>bstain**;
b) **Impairment in <u>B</u>ehavioral control**;
c) **<u>C</u>raving**; or increased "hunger" for drugs or rewarding experiences;
d) **<u>D</u>iminished recognition of significant problems** with one's behaviors and interpersonal relationships; and
e) **A dysfunctional <u>E</u>motional response**.

The **power of external cues** to trigger craving and drug use, as well as to increase the frequency of engagement in other potentially addictive behaviors, is also a characteristic of addiction, with the hippocampus being important in memory of previous euphoric or dysphoric experiences, and with the amygdala being important in having motivation concentrate on selecting behaviors associated with these past experiences.

Although some believe that the difference between those who have addiction, and those who do not, is the *quantity* or *frequency* of alcohol/drug use, engagement in addictive behaviors (such as gambling or spending), or exposure to other external rewards (such as food or sex), a characteristic aspect of addiction is the *qualitative way* in which the individual responds to such exposures, stressors and environmental cues. A particularly pathological aspect of *the way* that persons with addiction pursue substance use or external rewards is that preoccupation with, obsession with and/or pursuit of rewards (e.g., alcohol and other drug use) persist despite the accumulation of adverse consequences. These manifestations can occur compulsively or impulsively, as a reflection of impaired control.

Persistent risk and/or recurrence of relapse, after periods of abstinence, is another fundamental feature of addiction. This can be triggered by exposure to rewarding substances and behaviors, by exposure to environmental cues to use, and by exposure to emotional stressors that trigger heightened activity in brain stress circuits.[4]

In addiction there is a significant impairment in executive functioning, which manifests in problems with perception, learning, impulse control, compulsivity, and judgment. People with addiction often manifest a lower readiness to change their dysfunctional behaviors despite mounting concerns expressed by significant others in their lives; and display an apparent lack of appreciation of the magnitude of cumulative problems and complications. The still developing frontal lobes of adolescents may both compound these deficits in executive functioning and predispose youngsters to engage in "high risk" behaviors, including engaging in alcohol or other drug use. The profound drive or craving to use substances or engage in apparently rewarding behaviors, which is seen in many patients with addiction, underscores the compulsive or avolitional aspect of this disease. This is the connection with "powerlessness" over addiction and "unmanageability" of life, as is described in Step 1 of 12 Steps programs.

Addiction is more than a behavioral disorder. Features of addiction include aspects of a person's behaviors, cognitions, emotions, and interactions with others, including a person's ability to relate to members of their family, to members of their community, to their own psychological state, and to things that transcend their daily experience.

Behavioral manifestations and complications of addiction, primarily due to impaired control, can include:

a) Excessive use and/or engagement in addictive behaviors, at higher frequencies and/or quantities than the person intended, often associated with a persistent desire for and unsuccessful attempts at behavioral control;

b) Excessive time lost in substance use or recovering from the effects of substance use and/or engagement in addictive behaviors, with significant adverse impact on social and occupational functioning (e.g. the development of interpersonal relationship problems or the neglect of responsibilities at home, school or work);

c) Continued use and/or engagement in addictive behaviors, despite the presence of persistent or recurrent physical or psychological problems which may have been caused or exacerbated by substance use and/or related addictive behaviors;

d) A narrowing of the behavioral repertoire focusing on rewards that are part of addiction; and

e) An apparent lack of ability and/or readiness to take consistent, ameliorative action despite recognition of problems.

Cognitive changes in addiction can include:

a) Preoccupation with substance use;
b) Altered evaluations of the relative benefits and detriments associated with drugs or rewarding behaviors; and
c) The inaccurate belief that problems experienced in one's life are attributable to other causes rather than being a predictable consequence of addiction.

Emotional changes in addiction can include:

a) Increased anxiety, dysphoria and emotional pain;
b) Increased sensitivity to stressors associated with the recruitment of brain stress systems, such that "things seem more stressful" as a result; and
c) Difficulty in identifying feelings, distinguishing between feelings and the bodily sensations of emotional arousal, and describing feelings to other people (sometimes referred to as alexithymia).

The emotional aspects of addiction are quite complex. Some persons use alcohol or other drugs or pathologically pursue other rewards because they are seeking "positive reinforcement" or the creation of a positive emotional state ("euphoria"). Others pursue substance use or other rewards because they have experienced relief from negative emotional states ("dysphoria"), which constitutes "negative reinforcement." Beyond the initial experiences of reward and relief, there is a **dysfunctional emotional state** present in most cases of addiction that is associated with the persistence of engagement with addictive behaviors. The state of addiction is not the same as the state of intoxication. When anyone experiences mild intoxication through the use of alcohol or other drugs, or when one engages non-pathologically in potentially addictive behaviors such as gambling or eating, one may experience a "high", felt as a "positive" emotional state associated with increased dopamine and opioid peptide activity in reward circuits. After such an experience, there is a neurochemical rebound, in which the reward function does not simply revert to baseline, but often drops below the original levels. This is usually not

251

consciously perceptible by the individual and is not necessarily associated with functional impairments.

Over time, repeated experiences with substance use or addictive behaviors are not associated with ever increasing reward circuit activity and are not as subjectively rewarding. Once a person experiences withdrawal from drug use or comparable behaviors, there is an anxious, agitated, dysphoric and labile emotional experience, related to suboptimal reward and the recruitment of brain and hormonal stress systems, which is associated with withdrawal from virtually all pharmacological classes of addictive drugs. While tolerance develops to the "high," tolerance does not develop to the emotional "low" associated with the cycle of intoxication and withdrawal. Thus, in addiction, persons repeatedly attempt to create a "high"--but what they mostly experience is a deeper and deeper "low." While anyone may "want" to get "high", those with addiction feel a "need" to use the addictive substance or engage in the addictive behavior in order to try to resolve their dysphoric emotional state or their physiological symptoms of withdrawal. Persons with addiction compulsively use even though it may not make them feel good, in some cases long after the pursuit of "rewards" is not actually pleasurable.[5] Although people from any culture may choose to "get high" from one or another activity, it is important to appreciate that addiction is not solely a function of choice. Simply put, addiction is not a desired condition. As addiction is a chronic disease, periods of relapse, which may interrupt spans of remission, are a common feature of addiction. It is also important to recognize that return to drug use or pathological pursuit of rewards is not inevitable.

Clinical interventions can be quite effective in altering the course of addiction. Close monitoring of the behaviors of the individual and contingency management, sometimes including behavioral consequences for relapse behaviors, can contribute to positive clinical outcomes. Engagement in health promotion activities which promote personal responsibility and accountability, connection with others, and personal growth also contribute to recovery. It is important to recognize that **addiction can cause disability or premature death, especially when left untreated or treated inadequately**.

The qualitative ways in which the brain and behavior respond to drug exposure and engagement in addictive behaviors are different at later stages of addiction than in earlier stages, indicating progression, which may not be overtly apparent. As is the case with other chronic diseases, the condition must be monitored and managed over time to:

a) Decrease the frequency and intensity of relapses;
b) Sustain periods of remission; and
c) Optimize the person's level of functioning during periods of remission.

In some cases of addiction, medication management can improve treatment outcomes. In most cases of addiction, the integration of psychosocial rehabilitation and ongoing care with evidence-based pharmacological therapy provides the best results. Chronic disease management is important for minimization of episodes of relapse and their impact. Treatment of addiction saves lives †

Addiction professionals and persons in recovery know the hope that is found in recovery. Recovery is available even to persons who may not at first be able to perceive this hope, especially when the focus is on linking the health consequences to the disease of addiction. **As in other health conditions, self-management, with mutual support, is very important in recovery from addiction**. Peer support such as that found in various "self-help" activities is beneficial in optimizing health status and functional outcomes in recovery. ‡

Recovery from addiction is best achieved through a combination of self-management, mutual support, and professional care provided by trained and certified professionals.

---

† See ASAM Public Policy Statement on **Treatment for Alcohol and Other Drug Addiction**, Adopted: May 01, 1980, Revised: January 01, 2010

‡ see ASAM Public Policy Statement on **The Relationship between Treatment and Self Help: A Joint Statement of the American Society of Addiction Medicine, the American Academy of Addiction Psychiatry, and the American Psychiatric Association**, Adopted: December 01, 1997

Explanatory footnotes:

1. The neurobiology of reward has been well understood for decades, whereas the neurobiology of addiction is still being explored. Most clinicians have learned of reward pathways including projections from the ventral tegmental area (VTA) of the brain, through the median forebrain bundle (MFB), and terminating in the nucleus accumbens (Nuc Acc), in which dopamine neurons are prominent. Current neuroscience recognizes that the neurocircuitry of reward also involves a rich bi-directional circuitry connecting the nucleus accumbens and the basal forebrain. It is the reward circuitry where reward is registered, and where the most fundamental rewards such as food, hydration, sex, and nurturing exert a strong and life-sustaining influence. Alcohol, nicotine, other drugs and pathological gambling behaviors exert their initial effects by acting on the same reward circuitry that appears in the brain to make food and sex, for example, profoundly reinforcing. Other effects, such as intoxication and emotional euphoria from rewards, derive from activation of the reward circuitry. While intoxication and withdrawal are well understood through the study of reward circuitry, understanding of addiction requires understanding of a broader network of neural connections involving forebrain as well as midbrain structures. Selection of certain rewards, preoccupation with certain rewards, response to triggers to pursue certain rewards, and motivational drives to use alcohol and other drugs and/or pathologically seek other rewards, involve multiple brain regions outside of reward neurocircuitry itself.

2. These five features are not intended to be used as "diagnostic criteria" for determining if addiction is present or not. Although these characteristic features are widely present in most cases of addiction, regardless of the pharmacology of the substance use seen in addiction or the reward that is pathologically pursued, each feature may not be equally prominent in every case. The diagnosis of addiction requires a comprehensive biological, psychological, social and spiritual assessment by a trained and certified professional.

3. In this document, the term "addictive behaviors" refers to behaviors that are commonly rewarding and are a feature in many cases of addiction. Exposure to these behaviors, just as occurs with exposure to rewarding drugs, is facilitative of the addiction process rather than causative of addiction. The state of brain anatomy and physiology is the underlying variable that is more directly causative of addiction. Thus, in this document, the term "addictive behaviors" does not refer to dysfunctional or socially disapproved behaviors, which can appear in many cases of addiction. Behaviors, such as dishonesty, violation of one's values or the values of others, criminal acts etc., can be a component of addiction; these are best viewed as complications that result from rather than contribute to addiction.

4. The anatomy (the brain circuitry involved) and the physiology (the neuro-transmitters involved) in these three modes of relapse (drug- or reward-triggered relapse vs. cue-triggered relapse vs. stress-triggered relapse) have been delineated through neuroscience research.

Relapse triggered by exposure to addictive/rewarding drugs, including alcohol, involves the nucleus accumbens and the VTA-MFB-Nuc Acc neural axis (the brain's mesolimbic dopaminergic "incentive salience circuitry"--see footnote 2 above). Reward-triggered relapse also is mediated by glutamatergic circuits projecting to the nucleus accumbens from the frontal cortex.

Relapse triggered by exposure to conditioned cues from the environment involves glutamate circuits, originating in frontal cortex, insula, hippocampus and amygdala projecting to mesolimbic incentive salience circuitry.

Relapse triggered by exposure to stressful experiences involves brain stress circuits beyond the hypothalamic-pituitary-adrenal axis that is well known as the core of the endocrine stress system. There are two of these relapse-triggering brain stress circuits – one originates in noradrenergic nucleus A2 in the lateral tegmental area of the brain stem and projects to the hypothalamus, nucleus accumbens, frontal cortex, and bed nucleus of the stria terminalis, and uses norepinephrine as its neurotransmitter; the other originates in the central nucleus of the amygdala, projects to the bed nucleus of the stria terminalis and uses corticotrophin-releasing factor (CRF) as its neurotransmitter.

5. Pathologically pursuing reward (mentioned in the Short Version of this definition) thus has multiple components. It is not necessarily the amount of exposure to the reward (e.g., the dosage of a drug) or the frequency or duration of the exposure that is pathological. In addiction, pursuit of rewards persists, despite life problems that accumulate due to addictive behaviors, even when engagement in the behaviors ceases to be pleasurable. Similarly, in earlier stages of addiction, or even before the outward manifestations of addiction have become apparent, substance use or engagement in addictive behaviors can be an attempt to pursue relief from dysphoria; while in later stages of the disease, engagement in addictive behaviors can persist even though the behavior no longer provides relief.

⫲**RICHER Press**
An Imprint of Richer Life, LLC

RICHER Press is a full service, specialty Trade publisher whose sole goal is to *shape thoughts and change lives for the better*. All of the books, eBooks and digital media we publish, distribute and market embrace our commitment to help maximize opportunities for personal growth and professional achievement.

To learn more visit
www.richerlifeassociates.com.

ALSO BY

Dawn V. Obrecht, M.D.

MISSION POSSIBLE
A Missionary Doctor's Journey of Healing

"Mission Possible" Has Been Nominated For a 2012 Montaigne Medal

The Montaigne Medal

Each year, the Eric Hoffer Award for books presents the Montaigne Medal to the most thought-provoking title(s). These are books that either illuminate, progress, or redirect thought. The Montaigne Medal is given in honor of the great French philosopher Michel de Montaigne, who influenced people such as William Shakespeare, René Descartes, Ralph Waldo Emerson, Friedrich Nietzsche, Jean-Jacques Rousseau, and Eric Hoffer.

Montaigne Medal
Eric Hoffer Award
Excellence in
Independent Publishing